W9-BEX-558

The Gourmet
indian cookbook

ISBN: 81-7436-299-1

Published in India by
Roli Books in arrangement
with Roli & Janssen
M-75 Greater Kailash II (Market)
New Delhi 110 048, India
Ph: ++91-11-29212271, 29212782,
29210886; Fax: ++91-11-29217185
E-mail: roli@vsnl.com
Website: rolibooks.com

Printed and bound at Singapore

Chef Arvind Saraswat

The Gourmet indian cookbook

Lustre Press
Roli Books

contents

foreword

The first time I met Arvind Saraswat and experienced his precious cooking skills was at the Taj Mahal Hotel, Mumbai (Bombay then), the hotel was and still is a hostelry to reckon with. It was when this young man engineered a seafood bonanza for me which was started with *Tiger Prawn Salad with Orange Reduction and black pepper dressing* and followed by my first ever taste of the *Lobster Thermidor* served in its own shell. It was a meal fit for the gods... Ooh! la! la!

It may sound childish, but thereafter, whenever I got a chance to get him to make *Thermidor* for me, I never let it pass. Without meaning to flatter him, each time, it was near perfect. I am quite sure, what I saw then made the basis for what he has achieved in his new book—*The Gourmet Indian Cookbook*, the like of which has never been seen before. Mercifully, he never fell into the trap of that ugly word, 'fusion'. We felt fusion was for music and perhaps some other art forms, but certainly not for food. He always said that, 'it is critical to maintain the purity of a cuisine for the best taste.' This was a rare attitude among Indian chefs, who were for some reason trying to be cute with the 6000-year-old cuisine, rich in legend and style.

He was one amongst a handful of young Turks who set new trends in Indian cuisine. Without meaning to get into a writer's hyperbole, it was obvious for me that Saraswat would inherit this ancient and legendary 'kingdom'.

This was also apparent to the mandarins who ran his company and treasured this young man of munificent skills for bigger things. They lost no time in rewarding him by sending him to the venerable Rendezvous, as *chef de cuisine* when he was all of 25-years-old at that time (in kitchen terms, a mere pup). Since that time, the Rendezvous was regarded as the finest eatery in the land.

Funny, but I who hate to see our young talent go overseas for a few bucks, remember asking myself, 'What is this guy doing here? He should be honing his magnificent skills with Bocuse, Ducasse or the Trois Gras brothers, or Roux brothers to become the first Indian to earn a michelin star.'

His real skills shone through to me when he generously helped me with my book, *Prashad— Cooking with Indian Masters*. At that time Indian food was great to taste, but missed out completely on visual appeal. Saraswat brought an element of internationalization in some of the chapters where his contribution was monumental.

The thought behind his current book took seed when Saraswat created a banquet in July 1993, hosted by Dr L M Singhvi, the then Indian High Commissioner in London in honour of the British Prime Minister, John Major at St James Court Hotel, London. Some of the delights served include*d Chicken Roundels with a Mint-flavoured Mousse and Green Lentil Sauce* and *A Combination of Gram flour Dumplings with Scalded Milk and Melon Sorbet*. The diners were astonished that the Indian food, then in vogue, could be served as elegantly as in other parts of the world.

Saraswat has also shown his innovative skills by marrying exotic, traditional Indian delicacies with western-style (I prefer to use the wor*d* 'international style presentation').

It is evident that eating styles through evolution have become universal and redefined and are thus not confined to regions and traditions. It is the first time in the history of Indian cuisine that he has taken our thoughts away from the controversy of regional food. The dishes featured in the book have an Indian character. The best of the pan-Indian dishes have been accommodated and elegantly introduced in one form or the other smartly—a step forward towards the national integration of our food.

A new version of Indian cuisine has evolved, with very specific changes in the style of presentation and portion. This has been done without tampering with the original taste of any of India's popular dishes. The traditional Indian cuisine has been transformed into a novel culinary adventure with the innovative use of herbs and spices, each dish is carefully orchestrated to create a visual impact—from the main ingredient to the accompaniment, and the garnish.

I would like to congratulate Arvind Saraswat for this tremendous work—the first of its kind. This book is an exception and a must for collectors of all hues—be it amateur cooks, housewives, students of catering colleges and, most importantly, his peers. It is a great culinary contribution to the kitchens of India ranging from super deluxe hotels, stand-alone restaurants to a humble home kitchen. It could well be described as the beginning of a great revolution aimed at making Indian food compete with international cuisines, be it in terms of visual-appeal, portion, presentation, balance, nutrition or satiety value.

The dishes showcased in the book are lighter, smaller in portion, and very skillfully displayed. In a rare departure from traditional Indian cooking, Saraswat has enhanced his cuisine by introducing lighter sauces the sweetness has been cut down and the fat content reduced, drastically, unlike heavy sauces laden with cashew nuts, almonds or poppy seeds. Many of the sauces are fruit based and have been upgraded so that they have an universal appeal.

Saraswat has trained and encouraged hundreds of young chefs and strongly believes in discipline. His cooking revolves around one important fact—dedication—which is an important factor in creating high standards and perfection in our cuisine. It will be a sad day when he takes off his *toque* and finally puts down his ladles and tongs, but, for a man who has given so much to this profession —his youth, family, time, and efforts, one can only stand back and give him a standing ovation for a job well-done with splendid aplomb.

With Saraswat, I hope Indian food will not only take a new direction, but a step forward, in the new millennium. Some of my favourite recipes that need to be tried and enjoyed again and again are *Treasure Trove, Mystic Swirl, Fire Fingers, Sea Splendour, Triple Sensation, Paneer Cache, Spiral Approach, Studded Platter, Golden Glory, Kaleidoscope,* and *Treasured Moments.* I have no words for the *Paan Sorbet. Paan*—an after meal digestive—transformed into a delicious minty ice cream. I will be surprised if the book is not seen on every shelf—home, college, or library. I would also like to take this opportunity to wish Saraswat good health and hope that he will come up with many more books in the future.

Bon appetit!

— Jiggs Kalra

the world of indian spices

Cuisine is an expression of a nation's soul and any understanding of Indian cuisine would have to take into account our diverse and fascinating spices. Their sensuous aromas and flavours enliven the palate, activate the tastebuds and heighten the enjoyment of gastronomic pleasures. They have been essential to the development of the personality of Indian cuisine and played an important role in the health and well-being of the body.

Our understanding of Indian cuisine cannot be complete without the knowledge of the full potential of spices, how to deal with them, the specific techniques involved in their preparation and the equipment needed on hand. We have an endless list of spices from which to choose and work with, but we cannot extract the desired results unless their qualities are understood.

Whole spices are roasted to enhance the flavour. The drying process is simple. Spices can be roasted in a dry pan over very low heat or in the oven, or can been done traditionally in the sun. Each spice should be roasted until it releases its unique aroma. A few minutes is all you need. If it is being dried in the sun, the process takes a few days. The spices should change to light brown but must never be burnt, otherwise those that contain oil, like cloves, nutmeg and cardamom, would lose the oil component which gives them their unique flavour. Besides, spices are easier to grind when roasted or dried.

The spices used in Indian cooking have preventive and curative properties giving them medicinal values as well. Cumin, coriander, nutmeg, fennel, and cardamom help digestion while cloves are known to prevent tooth decay.

Asafoetida *(hing)*: Obtained in the form of a resinous gum from a plant that grows mainly in Afghanistan and Iran. Despite its disagreeable odour, a minuscule amount, attached to the lid of the vessel, can add a very distinct and yet agreeable flavour. A must in Gujarati cooking. Asafoetida is used in very small quantities to prevent flatulence.

Aromatic ginger *(saunth)*: Though aromatic ginger provides a distinct flavour and aroma, it is rarely used. Available fresh and dried, this cannot substitute ginger under any circumstances.

Black cumin *(shahi jeera)*: Despite its Hindi description, this is not the real cumin. It is aromatic, peppery and has a flavour that is different from cumin.

Bay leaves *(tej patta)*: Used exclusively in North Indian cuisine for flavouring; bay leaves are discarded after use.

Cardamom (*elaichi*): Of all the spices in the world, only saffron is more expensive than cardamom. It is grown mainly in India and Sri Lanka and comes in two sizes—*choti*, which is green, and *badi* or *moti*, which is dark brown. While the larger cardamom is an essential part of traditional garam masala, the smaller one is used for desserts and *pulao*. Again, while the latter can replace the larger, the reverse is not possible.

Carom seeds *(ajwain)*: Similar to parsley seeds, carom seeds have a thyme-like flavour. An essential

From Left to Right

Top Row: Black cumin, Onion seeds, Mango powder, Mace, Poppy seeds, Mustard seeds
Bottom Row: Asafoetida, Dry red chillies, Carom seeds, Nutmeg, Cinnamon, Coriander seeds

part of the vegetarian diet (rich in protein), the seeds also provide the predominant flavour in crisp-fried snacks like *samosa* and *pakora*. Carom seeds have strong medicinal properties, especially for stomach disorders.

Coriander (*dhaniya*) seeds: Dried and ground, coriander is the mainstay of Indian cookery.

Curry leaves (*kadhi patta*): Curry leaves are an essential ingredient in almost all curries. Though these are often dried before being sold, curry leaves are available in such abundance—the tree grows exclusively in many parts of Asia—that it is also used fresh, in which case it is fried until it turns crisp as the first step in preparing a curry.

Cloves (*laung*): Another prized spice, cloves are an essential ingredient in garam masala. The dried flower bud of an evergreen tropical tree, which grows mostly in south-east Asia, it was first used in China over 2,000 years ago. The oil that is derived from the buds acts as an effective antiseptic—it has phenol, which prevents putrefaction and is an excellent mouth-freshener. Cloves thus help in the preservation of food.

Cinnamon (*dalchini*): Real cinnamon is found in Sri Lanka only. What is grown in India, Indonesia and Myammar is cassia. It is similar, but a lot cheaper. Though cassia is much stronger in flavour, it lacks the delicacy of the real cinnamon. Both are used for sweet and savoury foods, yet cinnamon goes better with desserts. Cinnamon is a pale, thin bark while cassia is darker and coarser.

Fennel (*saunf*): Fennel is also known as 'sweet cumin' because of its appearance. Its flavour is akin to that of licorice. Roasted fennel is served after a meal to freshen the mouth. Fennel water helps in digestion.

Fenugreek (*methi*): Small, squat, squarish, and brownish-beige in colour, fenugreek seeds have a slightly bitter flavour. A must in the preparation of pickles.

Gold and Silver leaves (*varak*): Like rose water, *varak*, too, is used on festive occasions, but unlike rose water, this can be used with almost every food. Gold leaves are a rarity for obvious reasons. It is claimed that *varak* has the qualities of an aphrodisiac and is not just an edible decoration.

Mango powder (*amchur*): It has a tangy quality that tickles the tastebuds and is used as a flavouring for *chaat* and other savouries.

Mace (*javitri*): A member of the nutmeg family, its fragrance though much more delicate, is similar to that of nutmeg. Again, like nutmeg, mace is used sparingly—only for meat and fish curries—as part of the garam masala. It can add a new dimension to *handi* cooking. Mace releases heat, so use very little of it in summer.

Mustard seeds (*rai*): A must for the masala used in pickles, black mustard seeds are smaller and more pungent than the yellow ones.

Nutmeg (*jaiphal*): A wonderfully aromatic spice, nutmeg is used rarely and in very small quantities as part of the traditional garam masala. Be warned: nutmeg, if excessively used, is poisonous.

Onion seeds (*kalonji*): Without these small, black and delightfully aromatic seeds, a *naan* would be just ordinary unleavened bread. Bengalis cannot think of cooking vegetables or fish without onion seeds.

Poppy seeds (*khus-khus*): White poppy seeds are to curries what flour and cornflour are to sauces—they are used as a thickening agent. Of course, poppy seeds have to be powdered for the purpose. Black poppy seeds are never used in gravies—their flavour is very different and would only ruin the curry. These seeds are used as garnish with Indian breads.

FROM LEFT TO RIGHT

TOP ROW: Curry leaves, Fennel, Silver leaves, Aromatic ginger, Turmeric powder, Tamarind
BOTTOM ROW: Cloves, Poppy seeds, Saffron, Green cardamoms, Fenugreek, White cumin

Rose water (*gulab jal*): Like vetivier, rose water is the diluted essence of rose petals. The essence is extracted with the help of steam distillation. It is also available as an essence and a concentrate. In the latter case, you have to be careful not to use too much of it. A favourite with *halwais*, rose water is sprinkled on most Indian sweets before they are packed.

Saffron (*kesar*): Prized for its supposed aphrodisiacal qualities, saffron is the world's most expensive spice. Its thread-like strands, obviously, have a saffron or dark orange hue and a delicate aroma, unlike any other spice. Saffron is used more extensively in North India than anywhere else in Asia. Grown in Kashmir, the quality of Indian saffron is as good as its Spanish cousin.

Sesame seeds (*til*): These beige coloured, unhulled seeds are an essential ingredient in *rewari, gajak, chikki* and other winter sweets, and often used to thicken gravies. They are best avoided in summer.

Tamarind (*imli*): Tamarind is a long, wide, bean-shaped fruit that grows on tropical trees. The main fruit is the pulp inside the brittle shell. Tamarind is dried before being sold and, before use, it is soaked in lukewarm water for 5-10 minutes until soft. It is squeezed until it dissolves in water and then the seeds and fibers are strained out.

Turmeric (*haldi*): This sunrise yellow spice may be called the Indian saffron, but the comparison is not accurate. The two, moreover, are not inter-changeable. In fact turmeric is a flavourless root, even though it is a common factor in almost all masalas.

Vetivier (*kewra*): Available as an essence or a concentrate, vetivier has a perfume stronger than jasmine and roses. It is also available as *kewra* water, which has, a much milder fragrance. This is because *kewra* is so strong that just a drop is enough to flavour the whole dish. *Kewra* flavouring is, however, reserved for festive and special occasions.

White cumin (*safed jeera*): Cumin is one of the most essential ingredients in any masala. Because of its appearance, it is often confused with caraway. The aroma, however, is completely different and one can never be a substitute for the other.

Aromatic Garam Masala: (Yield: 7oz/200 gm)

Take 20 tsp cumin *(jeera)* seeds, 6 tbsp black peppercorns *(sabut kali mirch)*, ½ tbsp cloves *(laung)*, 5½ tbsp green cardamoms *(choti elaichi)*, ½ tbsp cinnamon *(dalchini)* sticks, 1 tsp mace *(javitri)*, and 2 tsp fennel *(saunf)*.

Put the ingredients individually in a grinder and make a fine powder. Sieve, mix and store in a sterilized, dry and airtight container.

Aromatic Tangy Masala: (Yield: 5¼ oz/150 gm)

Take 1½ tbsp black peppercorns *(sabut kali mirch)*, 1½ tbsp white peppercorns *(sabut safed mirch)*, 5 tsp black salt (pound, if using grinder), 10 tsp cumin *(jeera)* seeds, 1 tsp carom seeds *(ajwain)*, 5 tsp dry mint *(pudina)* leaves, 1 tsp tartric (pound, if using grinder), 5 tbsp mango powder *(amchur)*, 2 tbsp salt, 2 tsp ginger powder *(saunth)*, and 2 tsp yellow chilli powder.

Put all the ingredients (except mango powder, salt, ginger powder, and yellow chilli powder) in a grinder and make a fine powder. Sieve, transfer to a clean, dry bowl. Add the remaining ingredients and mix well. Sieve and store in a sterilized dry and airtight container.

---

basic recipes

Boiled Onion Paste: (Yield: 2.2 lb/1 kg)

Take 2.2 lb/1 kg onions, peeled, washed, roughly chopped; 3 bay leaves *(tej patta)*, and 3 black cardamoms *(badi elaichi)*.

Put the onions in a pan, add bay leaves, black cardamoms, and 5 cups water, bring to the boil; simmer until onions are transparent and the liquid has evaporated. Transfer to a blender and make a fine purée. Cool and refrigerate.

Ajwain Crispies: (Yield: 4½ oz/125 gm)

Take 10 tbsp flour *(maida)*, salt to taste, a pinch of carom *(ajwain)* seeds, 1½ tbsp ghee, and groundnut oil for frying.

Mix f lour, salt, and carom seeds together. Make a well in the mixture, add melted ghee and rub between the palms. Add cold water (2½ tbsp approximately) and make a tight dough. (Do not over knead.) Roll into a thin sheet and cut the dough into match-stick size. Heat the oil in a pan and deep-fry the match-sticks until golden brown and crisp. Remove and spread over an absorbent paper.

Sun-dried Tomatoes: (Yield: 10½ oz/300 gm)

Take 2.2 lb/1 kg tomatoes, quartered, pulp removed, 1 tsp salt, 2 tsp balsamic vinegar *(sirka)*, 2 tbsp olive oil, and 5 tbsp green coriander *(hara dhaniya)*, chopped.

Flatten the tomatoes. Sprinkle salt and put them in a moderately hot oven for 45 minutes at 150°C/300°F or until dry and crisp. Mix vinegar, oil, and green coriander together. Sprinkle over the tomatoes. Serve warm.

Crisp Spinach: (Yield: 5¼ oz/150 gm)

Take 1.1 lb/500 gm spinach *(palak)*, julienned and groundnut oil for frying.

Heat the oil in a deep pan; add spinach and fry over medium heat until crisp. Remove and spread over an absorbent paper. Store in an airtight container.

Spinach Chlorophyll: (Yield: 10½ oz/300 gm)

Take 4.4 lb/2 kg spinach (*palak*) and a pinch of soda bicarbonate.

Bring enough water to the boil; add soda bicarbonate and spinach and cook for 2-3 minutes. Remove, drain and put in iced water immediately. Drain, squeeze and put in a blender, add water (1½ cups approximately) and make a fine purée. Add water (15 cups approximately) and bring to the boil. Reduce heat and remove the chlorophyll gently floating over the top. Cool, cover and refrigerate.

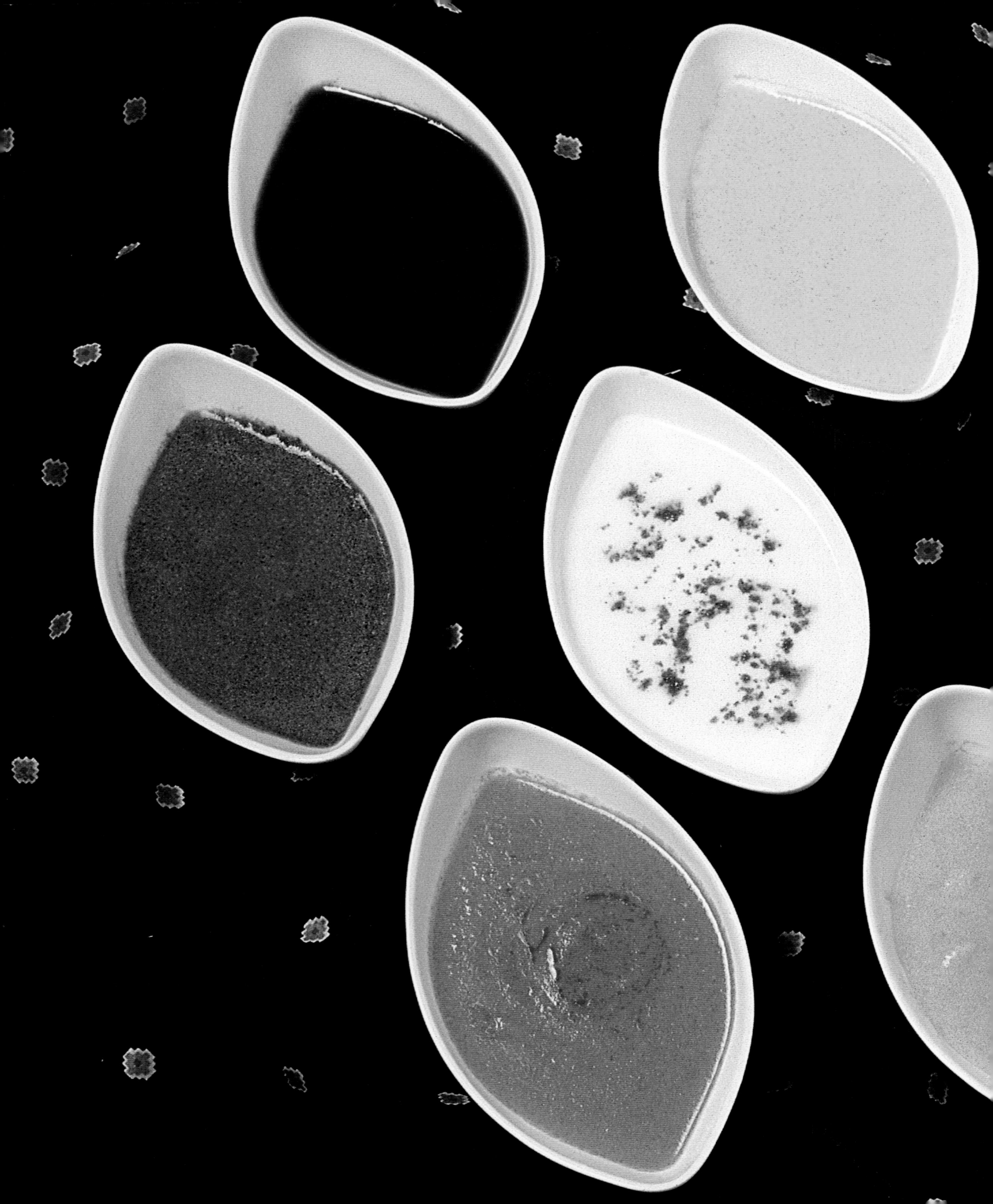

Sour Yoghurt Sauce: (Yield: 2.2 lb/1 kg)

Ingredients:

2.2 lb/1 kg sour yoghurt *(dahi)*, a day old, 3½ tbsp gram flour *(besan)*, 1 tsp turmeric *(haldi)* powder, ¼ cup groundnut oil, 8 dry red chillies *(sookhi lal mirch)*, 1 tsp fenugreek *(methi)* seeds, 1 tbsp coriander *(dhaniya)* seeds, 1 tsp cumin *(jeera)* seeds, ½ tsp mustard seeds *(rai)*, 10 curry leaves *(kadhi patta)*, 2 oz/56 gm tomato concasse, 4 tbsp green coriander *(hara dhaniya)*, chopped, and salt to taste.

Procedure:

- Put yoghurt, gram flour, and turmeric powder in a pan, add 7½ cups water and bring to the boil over medium heat, stirring continuously. Cook for 30 minutes.
- Heat the oil in a frying pan; add dry red chillies, stir. Add the remaining ingredients, stir for a minute and pour over the yoghurt sauce. Cover and keep aside for 15-20 minutes. Return to heat and bring the mixture to the boil again. Remove from heat and strain. Bring to the boil again. Adjust the consistency.
- The sauce should have a light coating consistency.

Tomato Butter Sauce: (Yield: 2.2 lb/1 kg)

Ingredients:

5.5 lb/2.5 kg red tomatoes, 5 cups water, 10 tbsp butter, 1 tsp cardamom-cinnamon-clove *(elaichi-dalchini-laung)*, 3½ tbsp ginger-garlic *(adrak-lasan)* paste, 1½ tsp red chilli powder, 1½ tsp dry fenugreek (in a muslin pouch), salt to taste, 2½ tbsp honey, 1½ cups cream, 2 tsp roux (butter and flour), and 1-2 drops of orange colour.

Procedure:

- Boil tomatoes and water together for 30 minutes. Remove and make a purée. Bring to the boil again and reduce to half over medium heat.
- Heat the butter in a pan; add cardamom-cinnamon-clove powder, stir. Add ginger- garlic paste, red chilli powder (dissolved in 2 tbsp water), tomato purée and add 3¼ cups water; bring to the boil over medium heat. Add the fenugreek pouch and salt; cook until the sauce is smooth. Remove the fenugreek pouch. Add honey and cream; bring to the boil. Pass through a fine strainer and bring to the boil again, add the roux and orange colour; mix. Adjust the consistency.
- The sauce should have a light coating consistency with a gloss/sheen on top.

Rogni Sauce: (Yield: 2.2 lb/1 kg)

Ingredients:

7 tbsp ghee, ½ tsp cardamom-cinnamon-cloves *(elaichi-dalchini-laung)*, 1¼ cups onions, chopped, 3½ tbsp ginger-garlic *(adrak-lasan)*, 1 tsp red chilli powder, 2 tsp coriander *(dhaniya)* powder, salt to taste, 3½ cups tomato purée, 5 cups lamb stock (see p.34), and 5 tsp roux (butter and flour).

Procedure:

- Heat the ghee in a pan; add cardamom-cinnamon-cloves and stir. Add onions and sauté over medium heat until golden brown. Add ginger-garlic paste, red chilli powder, coriander powder, and salt (all dissolved in 4 tbsp water); stir for a minute. Add tomato purée and cook until the ghee appears on the surface. Now add the lamb stock and boil for 5 minutes. Pass through a fine strainer. Bring to the boil again and add roux and mix. Adjust the consistency.
- The sauce should have a sheen and a smooth reddish-brown colour.

Cashew/Shahi Sauce: (Yield: 2.2 lb/1 kg)

Ingredients:

7 tbsp ghee, ½ tsp cardamom-cinnamon-clove *(elaichi-dalchini-laung)*, 3½ tbsp ginger-garlic *(adrak-lasan)* paste, 2 cups boiled onion paste (see p.13), 2 cups yoghurt *(dahi)*, beaten, 7 tbsp cashew nuts *(kaju)*, quick deep-fried until light brown, drained and made into a fine paste with 2½ cups water, 1 tsp white pepper *(safed mirch)* powder, dissolved in ¼ cup water, salt to taste, and ½ cup cream.

Procedure:

- Heat the ghee in a pan; add cardamom-cinnamon-cloves and stir over medium heat. Add ginger-garlic paste (dissolved in 4 tbsp water) and stir for a minute. Add boiled onion paste and stir for another 3-4 minutes. Now add yoghurt and continue stirring constantly until the ghee appears on the surface. Reduce heat, add cashew nut paste, white pepper powder, salt, and cook for 3-4 minutes. Add 2 cups water and bring to the boil. Add cream, bring to the boil again and remove. Pass through a fine strainer. Adjust the consistency.
- The sauce should have a coating consistency.

Saffron Sauce: (Yield: 2.2 lb/1 kg)

Ingredients:

2.2 lb/1 kg cashew/*shahi* sauce (see p.17) and a pinch of saffron *(kesar)*, dissolved in 2 tbsp water.

procedure:

Heat the cashew/*shahi* sauce in a pan over low heat; add saffron and continue to boil for a minute. Adjust the consistency.

Sweet Date and Tamarind Sauce: (Yield: 14 oz/400 gm)

Ingredients:

7 oz/200 gm dates *(khajoor)*, 7 oz/200 gm tamarind *(imli)*, 10½ oz/300 gm jaggery *(gur)*, 3 tsp cumin *(jeera)* powder, roasted, salt to taste, ½ tsp fennel *(saunf)* powder, ½ tsp ginger powder *(amchur)*, ½ tsp black salt, and ½ tsp red chilli powder.

Procedure:

Soak tamarind and dates in 5 cups water for 3-4 hours. Extract the pulp and juice, discard the seeds. Add jaggery, bring to the boil, stir until jaggery is dissolved and the sauce is of a coating consistency. Remove, add the remaining ingredients, stir and pass through a fine strainer. Cool, adjust the consistency.

Spinach Sauce: (Yield: 2.2 lb/1 kg)

Ingredients:

4 cups cashew/*shahi* sauce, 1½ cups spinach green chlorophyll (see p.13), and 1 tsp dry fenugreek powder *(kasoori methi)*.

Procedure:

Heat the cashew/*shahi* sauce in a pan over low heat. Add ½ cup water and bring to the boil. Add fenugreek powder and simmer for a minute. Add chlorophyll, adjust the consistency, stir and remove (use immediately, otherwise the green colour will change into a dull colour).

Mint and Coriander Sauce: (Yield: 21 oz/600 gm)

Ingredients:

5 tbsp mint *(pudina)*, without stems, chopped, ½ cup green coriander *(hara dhaniya)*, without stems, chopped, 10 green chillies, chopped, 1 tsp raw mango paste or 2 tbsp dry mango powder *(amchur)*, 1 tbsp lemon *(nimbu)* juice, salt to taste, 1½ cups yoghurt *(dahi)*, beaten, 1 tsp aromatic tangy masala (see p.12), and breakfast sugar (optional).

Procedure:

Put mint, green coriander, green chillies, and raw mango paste or dry mango powder, lemon juice, and ¾ cup chilled water in a blender and make a very fine purée. Add the remaining ingredients, stir, pass through a strainer and cool. It should have a coating consistency. Add sugar if the yoghurt is sour.

Cumin Yoghurt Sauce: (Yield: 2.2 lb/1 kg)

Ingredients:

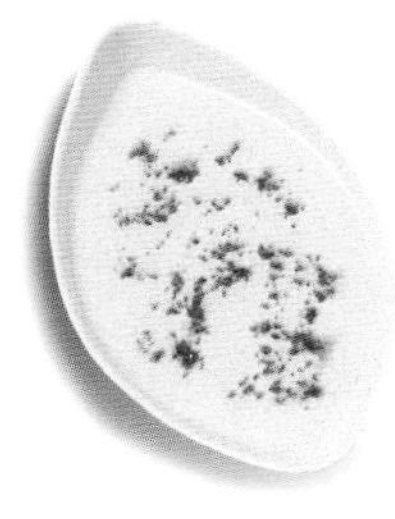

2.2 lb/1 kg yoghurt *(dahi)*, 3 tbsp breakfast sugar, 2 tsp cumin *(jeera)* powder, roasted, salt to taste, 1-2 drops cardamom *(elaichi)* essence or a pinch of cardamom powder.

Procedure:

Beat the yoghurt, add water and the remaining ingredients. Stir and pass through a strainer. Cool. The sauce should have a coating consistency. The quantity of water used will vary depending upon the consistency of the beaten yoghurt.

Tomato Chutney: (Yield: 14 oz/400 gm)

Ingredients:

3.3 lb/1.5 kg red tomatoes (concasse), 7 tbsp groundnut oil, 5 green chillies, chopped, 1 tsp red chilli powder, 2 tsp sugar, salt to taste, 5 curry leaves *(kadhi patta)*, 2 dry red chilli flakes, ½ tsp mustard *(sarson)* powder, and ½ tsp onion seed powder *(kalonji)*.

Procedure:

- Heat 6 tbsp oil in a pan; add tomatoes, bring to the boil over medium heat. Add green chillies, red chilli powder, sugar, and salt; cook until the ghee appears on the surface. Heat the remaining oil in a pan; add curry leaves and chilli flakes, stir over low heat, remove, add the remaining ingredients, stir and pour over tomato chutney; mix well. Adjust the consistency. It should have a soft pasty consistency.

soups and appetizers

Tangy Tomato Treat

Yield: 4 portions

Delicately flavoured tomato soup with a green pea timbale.

Ingredients:

Tomatoes, coarsely chopped	2.2 lb/1 kg
Butter	2 tsp
Green cardamoms *(choti elaichi)*	10-12
Cinnamon *(dalchini)* sticks	4-6
Bay leaves *(tej patta)*	2
Cloves *(laung)*	10-12
Garlic *(lasan)*, coarsely chopped	1 tbsp
Green chillies	1 tsp
Ginger *(adrak)*, coarsely chopped	1 tbsp
Onions, sliced	5 tbsp
Sugar and salt to taste	
Green coriander *(hara dhaniya)*, with stalks	1½ cups
Roux	5 tsp
Orange colour (optional)	a few drops

For the green pea timbale:
(Yield: 4 timbales)

Green peas *(mutter)*, boiled, crushed	5¼ oz/150 gm
Butter	2 tsp
Onions, chopped	2 tsp
Green chillies, chopped	1 tsp
Ginger, chopped	1 tsp
Mint *(pudina)*, chopped	1 tbsp
Salt to taste	
Egg white	1
Tomato, cut into ½" roundels	4 pieces

Procedure:

- Heat the butter in a pan; add whole spices and stir. Add garlic, green chillies, and ginger; sauté over medium heat for a minute. Add onions and sauté until transparent. Add tomatoes and sauté over medium heat for 8 10 minutes. Add 7 cups water; bring to the boil. Add sugar and salt and simmer for 30 minutes. Remove the scum.
- Add green coriander and simmer for 5 minutes; strain. Bring to the boil again and reduce to 4 cups. Add the roux and orange colour; stir.
- **For the green pea timbale:** Heat the butter, add onions, green chillies, and ginger; sauté over medium heat for 2 minutes. Add green peas and sauté for a minute. Add mint and salt; stir and blend along with the egg white to a smooth paste. Pour the mixture into 4 greased timbales (2" diameter x ¾" height), cover with a silver foil and steam for 5-6 minutes. Demould.

Presentation:

Place a green pea timbale in the centre of a soup plate and pour the soup gently. Garnish with a tomato roundel on the timbale. Serve warm.

Perfect Duo

Yield: 4 portions

A unique duet of golden fried rice cake and potato bar stuffed with a mixture of dates and walnuts with mint and coriander sauce accompanied by cumin yoghurt and sweet date and tamarind sauces.

Ingredients:

For the steamed rice cake (*idli*):
(Yield: 2.2 lb/1 kg)

Black gram *(urad dal)*, split, washed	7 oz/200 gm
Idli rawa	9 oz/250 gm
Salt to taste	
Idli bars 3½"x1"x1"	4
Potato bars 3½"x1"x1"	4
Groundnut oil for frying	
Cumin yoghurt sauce (see p.19)	8 tbsp
Mint and coriander sauce (see p.19)	4 tbsp
Dates & walnuts, chopped	2 tsp
Sweet date and tamarind sauce (see p.18)	8 tbsp

For the garnishing:

Cucumbers *(khira)*, carved into flowers (see p.123)	4
Tomatoes, carved into wings (see p.124)	8

Procedure:

- **For the steamed rice cake:** Soak black gram and *idli rawa* separately for 1 hour. Drain. Blend the black gram in a blender/wet grinder and make a smooth paste. Squeeze the extra water from the soaked *rawa* through a muslin. Mix with the dal paste and allow to ferment for 5-6 hours in a warm place. Season with salt.
- Pour the batter in a greased mould (10"x5"x4") and steam for 30-35 minutes. Remove, demould and cool. Cut into 3½"x1"x1" pieces with a sharp knife.
- Cut large potatoes into 3½"x1"x1" pieces with a knife.
- Make ¼" incision on all sides of the *idli* and potato bars leaving a thin wall on the sides. Scoop out ¼" deep. Blanch the potato bars.
- Heat the oil and fry the bars until golden brown. Remove, cool and dip in the cumin yoghurt sauce and drain the extra cumin yoghurt sauce by inverting the bars. Fill the bars with mint and coriander sauce mixed with dates and walnut in both the bars.

Presentation:

Spread 1½ tbsp of cumin yoghurt sauce and 1½ tbsp of sweet date and tamarind sauce half and half on a serving plate. Arrange an *idli* bar on the cumin yoghurt sauce and a potato bar on the sweet date and tamarind sauce. Garnish with cucumber flower and 2 tomato wings on the top of the plate.

Paneer Cache

Yield: 4 portions

Flaky Indian pastry filled with spiced cottage cheese served with cumin yoghurt sauce and laced with date and tamarind sauce.

Ingredients:

For the filling:	
Cottage cheese (*paneer*), diced	4 oz/120 gm
Ghee	2 tsp
Onions, diced	5 tsp
Turmeric (*haldi*) powder	½ tsp
Tomatoes, diced	5 tsp
Aromatic tangy masala (see p.12)	½ tsp
Cumin (*jeera*) powder	a pinch
Salt to taste	
Cashew/*Shahi* sauce (see p.17)	1 tbsp
Green coriander (*hara dhaniya*), chopped	1 tsp
For the flaky pastry:	
Flour (*maida*)	10 tbsp
Ghee	1¼ tbsp
Carom seeds (*ajwain*)	a pinch
Salt to taste	
Groundnut oil for frying	
For the garnishing:	
Cumin yoghurt sauce (see p.19)	16 tbsp
Sweet date and tamarind sauce (see p.18)	8 tbsp
Mint (*pudina*)	4 sprigs

Procedure:

- **For the filling:** Heat the ghee in a pan; sauté the onions over medium heat until transparent. Add turmeric powder, stir; add tomatoes and sauté for 2 minutes. Add cottage cheese, aromatic tangy masala, cumin powder, salt, cashew sauce, and green coriander; mix well. Remove, cool and divide the mixture into 4 equal portions.
- **For the flaky pastry:** Mix all the ingredients in a bowl; add approximately 2½ tbsp water and make a tight dough. Divide the dough into 4 equal portions and roll each portion into a 7″ disc. Cut 1½″ frill on the periphery with the tip of a knife. Wet the rolled pastry, place a portion of the filling in the centre and enfold. Press just below the frills to allow them to sprout like a lotus flower.
- Heat the ghee in a pan; deep-fry the pastries over low heat until golden brown. Remove and drain on paper towels.

Presentation:

Spread the cumin yoghurt sauce on the base of a plate. Dip two rings of 7″ and 5″ diameter in the date and tamarind sauce and then place over the cumin yoghurt sauce. Remove the rings. Make a design as shown in the photograph. Place the flaky pastry in the centre of the plate and arrange a mint sprig on the side.

Bounty Basket

Yield: 4 portions

A vegetarian delight of cottage cheese and morels served with tangy tomato sauce and garnished with pastry bows.

Ingredients:

Cottage cheese *(paneer)*, cut into 1¾"x1½" cylinders	4/1¾ oz/50 gm each
Tomato butter sauce (see p.16)	8 tbsp
Fenugreek *(methi)* powder	a pinch
Fennel-cardamom *(saunf-elaichi)* powder	a pinch
Seasoning to taste	
Mint and coriander sauce (see p.19)	6 tbsp
For the pastry bows:	
Flour *(maida)*	6 tbsp
Ghee	2 tsp
Carom seeds *(ajwain)*	a pinch
Salt to taste	
Groundnut oil for frying	
For the morels:	
Dry morels, medium-sized	6
Butter	2 tbsp
Onions, chopped	2 tsp
Green chillies, chopped	½ tsp
Ginger *(adrak)*, chopped	½ tsp
Cottage cheese, mashed	1 oz/28 gm
Green coriander *(hara dhaniya)*, chopped	1 tsp
Wholemilk fudge *(khoya)*, mashed	1 oz/28 gm
Salt to taste	
Saffron *(kesar)* sauce (see p.18)	2 tbsp

Procedure:

- Make a round hole (½" diameter and ½" deep) in the centre of the cottage cheese cylinders. Heat the tomato butter sauce in a pan; add spices and seasoning; mix. Add the cylinders and cook for 2 minutes. Remove and drain the extra sauce. Fill the hole with 1 tsp of mint and coriander sauce.
- **For the pastry bows:** Mix all the ingredients in a bowl; add approximately 1 tbsp water and make a semi-hard dough. Roll the dough out into a thin sheet and cut into 2"x¾"-long strips. Press the strip from the centre to make a bow shape. Heat the oil in a pan; deep-fry the pastry bows until golden brown. Remove.
- **For the morels:** Soak the morels for 30 minutes. Drain, trim the edges and cut each into half. Heat 1 tbsp butter in a pan; add the onions and sauté over medium heat until transparent. Add green chillies and ginger; sauté. Add cottage cheese and sauté for a minute. Remove, cool and add green coriander, wholemilk fudge, and salt; mix well. Stuff the morels with this mixture.
- Heat the remaining butter in a pan; sauté the stuffed morels. Serve warm.

Presentation:

Put 1 tbsp of mint and coriander sauce in the centre of the plate and arrange the cooked cottage cheese on top. Pour ½ tbsp saffron sauce on three sides of the plate. Arrange the three pastry bows on the sauce and three stuffed morels alternatively.

Captivating Conch

Yield: 4 portions

Maize flour savouries filled with tasty chick peas complemented with saffron and tomato butter sauces.

Ingredients:

For the maize shells:	
Maize flour (*makki ka atta*)	3½ oz/100 gm
Flour (*maida*)	1 oz/28 gm
Groundnut oil	1 tbsp
Salt to taste	
Groundnut oil for deep-frying	
For the filling:	
Chick peas (*kabuli chana*), boiled, crushed	5 oz/140 gm
Ghee	4 tsp
Garlic (*lasan*) paste	½ tsp
Red chilli powder	½ tsp
Coriander (*dhaniya*) powder	½ tsp
Tomatoes, chopped	3½ tbsp
Green chillies, chopped	½ tsp
Ginger (*adrak*), finely chopped	½ tsp
Aromatic tangy masala (see p.12)	a pinch
Lemon (*nimbu*) juice	a few drops
Salt to taste	
Green coriander (*hara dhaniya*), chopped	½ tsp
For the garnishing:	
Saffron (*kesar*) sauce (see p.18)	8 tbsp
Tomato butter sauce (see p.16)	8 tbsp
Green coriander	12 sprigs

Procedure:

- **For the maize shells:** Mix maize flour with flour, oil, salt, and 3 tbsp water; knead into a tight dough. Divide into 12 portions and line the small tartlet moulds. Deep-fry the shells along with the tin tartlet moulds until golden brown and crisp. Remove the maize shells from the tin moulds gently and use as required.
- **For the filling:** Heat the ghee in a pan; add garlic paste and stir over medium heat for 10 seconds. Add red chilli powder and coriander powder; stir. Add tomatoes, green chillies, and ginger; cook for 2-3 minutes. Now add the chick peas and stir for 2 minutes. Add approximately 2 tbsp water and stir.
- Add aromatic tangy masala, lemon juice, salt, and green coriander; mix well. Remove. Divide into 12 equal portions. Fill the maize shells with this mixture.

Presentation:

Pour 2 tbsp tomato butter sauce on the bottom of the plate and 2 tbsp saffron sauce on the top of the plate, make designs as shown in the photograph. Arrange the filled shells in a line and place a coriander sprig under each shell. (See photograph on p.20)

Sunny Sea

Yield: 4 portions

A hot 'n' sour yoghurt and gram flour soup set off with tangy and crisp okra.

Ingredients:

Sour yoghurt *(dahi)*, one day old	28 oz/800 gm
Gram flour *(besan)*	4 tbsp
Turmeric *(haldi)* powder	1 tsp
For the tempering:	
Butter	2 tbsp
Dry red chillies *(sookhi lal mirch)*	6
Fenugreek *(methi)* seeds	1 tsp
Mustard seeds *(rai)*	1 tsp
Coriander *(dhaniya)* seeds	2 tsp
Cumin *(jeera)* seeds	2 tsp
Curry leaves *(kadhi patta)*	10
Green coriander *(hara dhaniya)*, chopped	5 tbsp
Tomato concasse	4 tbsp
Salt to taste	
For the garnishing:	
Crisp okra (see p.92)	1½ oz/40 gm

Procedure:

- Mix yoghurt, gram flour, and turmeric powder in a pan. Add approximately 5 cups water; stir and bring to the boil. Reduce the heat and simmer for 20 minutes, stirring continuously.
- **For the tempering:** Heat the butter in a frying pan; add dry red chillies and sauté for 10 seconds. Add the remaining ingredients (except salt) and sauté for a minute. Add 2-3 ladles of the yoghurt soup and then pour the tempered mixture into the pan. Cover and rest for 15 minutes. Strain, bring to the boil and add salt. Adjust the soup to a pouring consistency. Serve hot.

Presentation:

Serve the yoghurt and gram flour soup in a soup plate sprinkled with crisp okra.

Almond Exotica

Yield: 4 portions

A mildly spiced cream of almond soup with saffron prawn wheel.

Ingredients:

Almond paste (made with 3½ oz almonds and 1 cup water)	10½ oz/300 gm
Butter	2 tbsp
Green cardamoms *(choti elaichi)*	3
Cloves *(laung)*	2
Cinnamon *(dalchini)* stick	1
Onions, chopped	4 tbsp
Garlic *(lasan)*, chopped	2 tsp
Ginger *(adrak)*, chopped	2 tsp
Flour *(maida)*	2 tsp
Tomatoes, chopped	2 tbsp
Cardamom-fennel *(elaichi-saunf)* powder	½ tsp
Cream	½ cup
Lemon *(nimbu)* juice	4 tsp
Salt to taste	
Saffron *(kesar)* extract	½ tsp
For the shrimp wheels: (Yield: 15 slices)	
Shrimps, fine mince, chilled	1 cup
Egg white, whisked	1
Salt to taste	
Ginger, chopped	½ tsp
Green coriander *(hara dhaniya)*, chopped	1 tbsp
Green chillies, chopped	½ tsp
Saffron extract	½ tsp
Spinach *(palak)*, large, blanched	3 oz/80 gm

Procedure:

- Heat the butter in a pan; add the whole spices and sauté over medium heat for 10 seconds. Add onions, garlic, and ginger; sauté until the onions turn transparent. Add flour and tomatoes; stir for a minute. Add cardamom-fennel powder and approximately 7 cups of water; bring to the boil, remove the scum and then simmer for 20 minutes. Add almond paste and cook for 5 minutes. Put in a blender and make a smooth purée. Pass through a strainer. Bring to the boil again; add cream, lemon juice, salt, and saffron extract; mix well. Serve hot.
- **For the shrimp wheels:** Mix shrimp mince with egg white and salt. Divide the mixture into 2:3 (i.e. ¼ cup and ¾ cup) portions. In the ¾ cup mixture, add ginger, green coriander, and green chillies; mix. Add saffron extract in the remaining ¼ cup mixture.
- Grease a silver foil, and spread spinach over it. Roll the saffron shrimp mixture like a cylinder and place it in the centre over the spinach leaves. Apply an egg wash. Roll the foil along with the mixture and tighten it from the side (1″ diameter).
- Steam the roll for 4-5 minutes. Remove, cool, peel off the foil gently and refrigerate the saffron shrimp roll. Spread a fresh silver foil, grease it and spread the other mixture evenly (¼″ thick). Egg wash and place the saffron shrimp roll in the middle. Gently roll the foil along with the mixture. Tighten from both ends. Steam the roll for 10-12 minutes. Remove, cool and peel off the foil. Slice the roll into ½″ thick slices.

Presentation:

Arrange 3 slices of the shrimp wheels on the 3 sides of a soup plate. Pour the soup gently. Serve hot.

Mystic Swirl

Yield: 4 portions

Lamb broth with brunoise of tomatoes, cucumber, lamb and mint, laced with sour yoghurt.

Ingredients:

Butter	2½ tbsp
Garlic *(lasan)*, chopped	2 tsp
Ginger *(adrak)*, chopped	2 tsp
Green cardamoms *(choti elaichi)*	3
Cloves *(laung)*	2
Cinnamon *(dalchini)* stick	1
Onions, chopped	4 tbsp
Flour *(maida)*	5 tsp
Curry leaves *(kadhi patta)*	5
Tomatoes, coarsely chopped	2 oz/56 gm
Potatoes, coarsely chopped	3½ oz/100 gm
Green coriander *(hara dhaniya)*, with stalks	3 tbsp
Lamb stock (see below)	7 cups
Cream	¼ cup
Lemon *(nimbu)* juice	1 tbsp
Cardamom-fennel *(elaichi-saunf)* powder	1 tsp
Salt to taste	
Saffron *(kesar)* extract	2 tsp
For the lamb stock:	
Lamb shin bone, cut into 3″ pieces	3.3 lb/1.5 kg
Onions, coarsely chopped	5 tbsp
Green cardamoms	4
Cloves	4
Cinnamon sticks	3
Bay leaves *(tej patta)*	3
Black peppercorns *(sabut kali mirch)*	20
Ginger, coarsely chopped	2 tbsp
Garlic	2 tbsp
For the garnishing:	
Lamb cubes, boiled	2 oz/56 gm
Tomatoes, cut into cubes	3 tbsp
Cucumber *(khira)*, cut into cubes	3 tbsp
Mint *(pudina)*, chopped	½ tbsp
Hung yoghurt *(dahi)*	4 tsp
Salt to taste	
Mint *(pudina)*	4 sprigs

Procedure:

- Heat the butter in a pan; add garlic, ginger, and whole spices; stir for a minute over medium heat. Add onions and sauté until brown. Add flour and curry leaves; stir for 2-3 minutes. Add tomatoes, potatoes, and green coriander; stir for 2-3 minutes. Add lamb stock (5 cups) and bring the mixture to the boil. Simmer for 15-20 minutes. Remove, put in a blender and make a smooth purée. Strain. Bring the purée to the boil in a pan; reduce heat and add cream, lemon juice, cardamom-fennel powder, and salt; mix well. Add saffron extract and stir.
- **For the lamb stock:** Put the bones in a roasting pan. Add onions and sauté until the bones are brown but not burnt. Transfer to a stock pot; add the remaining ingredients and approximately 35 cups water. Boil for 2 hours and strain. (Yield: 7½ cups)

Presentation:

Mix the garnish ingredients (except mint) together. Divide into 4 equal portions. Put a portion in a mould and demould in the centre of a soup plate. Pour the hot soup gently. Garnish with a mint sprig in the centre.

Treasure Trove

Yield: 4 portions

Spicy pickled shrimps on crisp spinach garnished with chilli butterfly prawns.

Ingredients:

Shrimps, peeled	7 oz/200 gm
Groundnut oil	2 tsp
Crisp spinach (see p.13)	¾ oz/20 gm
For the pickling paste:	
Cumin *(jeera)* seeds	2 tsp
Cloves *(laung)*	20
Black peppercorns *(sabut kali mirch)*	5
Cinnamon *(dalchini)* sticks	2
Ginger *(adrak)*, peeled, chopped	4 tsp
Garlic *(lasan)*, peeled	1 tbsp
Tamarind *(imli)*, seedless	1 oz/28 gm
Salt	1 tsp
Sugar	1 tbsp
Turmeric *(haldi)* powder	1 tsp
Dry red Kashmiri chillies	1½ oz/40 gm
Malt vinegar *(sirka)*	1½ cups
For the pickling sauce:	
Groundnut oil	¾ cup
Onions, chopped	7 tbsp
Ginger, chopped	2 tsp
Curry leaves *(kadhi patta)*	10
Tomato ketchup	1 cup
Jaggery *(gur)*	2 oz/56 gm
Salt to taste	
For the turmeric chilli prawns:	
Prawns, peeled with tail on	12
Turmeric powder	½ tsp
Red chilli powder	a pinch
Salt to taste	
Lemon *(nimbu)* juice	1½ tbsp
Groundnut oil	½ cup

Procedure:

- **For the pickling paste:** Put all the pickling ingredients in a blender and make a smooth paste. (Yield: 1½ cups)
- **For the pickling sauce:** Heat the oil (keep 1 tbsp aside) in a pan; add onions, ginger, and curry leaves; sauté over medium heat until the onions turn light golden brown. Add tomato ketchup and stir. Now add the pickling paste and approximately 2½ cups water and cook for 10 minutes or until the sauce is smooth. Add jaggery and stir until dissolved. Remove, cool and refrigerate. (Yield: 3½ cups)
- Heat the oil in a pan; add the shrimps and sauté for a minute over medium heat. Add 8-10 tbsp of pickling sauce and stir for 2 minutes. Divide into 4 portions and serve warm.
- **For the turmeric chilli prawns:** Shape the prawns like a butterfly. Take out the tail from the underside of the prawn in the centre. Wrap the tail with a silver foil. Marinate the prawns with turmeric powder, red chilli powder, salt, and lemon juice for 30 minutes.
- Heat the oil in a pan; add the prawns and place the pan in a moderately hot oven for 2 minutes. Remove the prawns from the pan, discard the silver foil and clean the tail. Serve warm.

Presentation:

Make a round bed of crisp spinach in the centre of a serving plate with the help of a ring (3″ diameter). Pour the pickled shrimps over the spinach. Arrange 3 turmeric chilli prawns on the 3 sides of the plate.

Golden Nuggets

Yield: 4 portions

Shrimp puffs complemented by a duet of tangy sauces, tamarind and mint together with cumin yoghurt sauce, garnished with sun-dried tomatoes.

Ingredients:

For the dumplings:

Flour *(maida)*	1¼ cups
Groundnut oil	1½ tbsp
Cornflour for dusting	

For the filling:

Shrimps, diced	6 oz/168 gm
Groundnut oil	3 tbsp
Garlic *(lasan)*, chopped	2 tsp
Onions, chopped	4 tbsp
Green chillies, chopped	1 tsp
Turmeric *(haldi)* powder	½ tsp
Tomato butter sauce (see p.16)	3½ tbsp

For the garnishing:

Mint and coriander sauce (see p.19)	4 tbsp
Cumin yoghurt sauce (see p.19)	4 tbsp
Sweet date and tamarind sauce (see p.18)	4 tsp
Sun-dried tomatoes (see p.13)	8-12
Green coriander *(hara dhaniya)*	4 sprigs

Procedure:

- **For the dumplings:** Make a tight dough with flour, oil, and approximately ¼ cup hot water. Divide the dough into 12 equal portions. Make balls and roll into thin sheets dusting with cornflour. Cut into discs (3½″ diameter and approximately 1 mm thick).
- **For the filling:** Heat the oil in a pan; add garlic, stir; add onions and sauté over medium heat until transparent. Add green chillies and turmeric powder; sauté. Add shrimps and sauté until cooked. Add tomato butter sauce and stir until the mixture is dry. Remove and cool. Divide the mixture into 12 equal portions.
- Place a portion of the shrimp mixture in the centre of a disc. Fold and join the edges together and pinch to make a fancy design. Heat the oil in a pan; deep-fry the dumplings until golden brown. Remove and drain. Serve warm.

Presentation:

Pour 1 tbsp mint and coriander sauce on the top of a serving plate. Arrange 3 shrimp puffs on it. At the bottom of the plate, pour 1 tbsp cumin yoghurt sauce and then 1 tsp sweet date and tamarind sauce over the cumin yoghurt sauce and make the desired design. Garnish with sun-dried tomatoes and green coriander sprigs.

Dainty Dumplings

Yield: 4 portions

Juicy chicken dumplings in a buttery tomato sauce served on a bed of herbed rice.

Ingredients:

For the chicken dumplings:	
Chicken mince (fine)	7 oz/200 gm
Onions, chopped	2 tbsp
Ginger *(adrak)*, chopped	2 tsp
Green chillies, chopped	1½ tsp
Cashew nut *(kaju)* paste	5 tsp
Aromatic tangy masala (see p.12)	1 tsp
Salt to taste	
*Chicken stock	1 cup
Tomato butter sauce (see p.16)	16 tbsp
Mace-cardamom *(javitri-elaichi)* powder	a pinch
For the herbed rice:	
Pressed rice *(chiwda)*, washed 2-3 times	2 oz/56 gm
Ghee	2 tbsp
Onions, chopped	4 tsp
Turmeric *(haldi)* powder	½ tsp
Green chillies, chopped	1 tsp
Cumin *(jeera)* powder	½ tsp
Green peas *(mutter)*, boiled	1½ oz/40 gm
Salt to taste	
Green coriander *(hara dhaniya)*, chopped	2 tbsp
Lemon *(nimbu)* juice	a few drops
For the garnishing:	
Bananas, cut into slices	12
Sweet date and tamarind sauce (see p.18)	8 tbsp
Cumin yoghurt sauce (see p.19)	8 tbsp

Procedure:

- **For the chicken dumplings:** Mix chicken mince with onions, ginger, green chillies, cashew nut paste, aromatic tangy masala, and salt. Knead well and divide the mixture into 12 equal portions. Shape each portion into balls with well-greased hands.
- ***For the chicken stock:** Put 3.3 lb/1.5 kg chicken bones in a stock pot. Add 5 tbsp chopped onions, 4 green cardamoms, 4 cloves, 3 cinnamon sticks, 3 bay leaves, 20 black peppercorns, and 30 cups water. Bring to the boil and simmer for 2 hours. Remove the scum occasionally and strain. (Yield: 10 cups)
- Heat the chicken stock and poach the chicken balls until cooked. Heat the tomato butter sauce in a frying pan; add the chicken balls and mace-cardamom powder; simmer for a minute. Adjust the sauce consistency. Serve warm.
- **For the herbed rice:** Heat the ghee in a pan; add onions and sauté over medium heat until transparent. Add turmeric powder, green chillies, cumin powder, and green peas; stir for a minute over medium heat.
- Add pressed rice, sprinkle water (just enough to make the rice soft), salt and green coriander; stir for a minute or two. When done remove, sprinkle lemon juice and divide the rice into 4 equal portions.

Presentation:

Place a ring (3″ diameter) and spread a portion of the herbed rice in the centre of the plate. Arrange 3 chicken dumplings over it. Dip 2 banana slices in sweet date and tamarind sauce and 1 banana slice in cumin yoghurt sauce and arrange them on the top of the plate. Pour 1 tbsp cumin yoghurt sauce at the bottom of the plate and 1 tsp sweet date and tamarind sauce on the cumin yoghurt sauce and make the desired design.

Fire Fingers

Yield: 4 portions

Glowing spicy red chicken fingers served with delicious gram flour yoghurt sauce, crisp spinach and tomato concasse flavoured with aromatic tangy masala.

Ingredients:

For the chicken fingers:
Chicken fingers (3″x½″) 20/7 oz/200 gm
Lemon *(nimbu)* juice 2 tbsp
Salt to taste
Flour *(maida)* for dusting

For the batter:
Flour 1 tsp
Cornflour 1 cup
Ginger-garlic *(adrak-lasan)* paste 1 tsp
Red chilli paste ½ tsp
Carom seeds *(ajwain)* a pinch
Red colour 1 tsp
Baking powder ½ tsp
Salt to taste
Groundnut oil for frying

For the garnishing:
Crisp spinach (see p.13) 1½ oz/40 gm
Sour yoghurt sauce (see p.16) 8 tbsp
Tomato concasse 3 oz/80 gm
Aromatic tangy masala (see p.12) a pinch

Procedure:

- **For the chicken fingers:** Marinate the chicken fingers with lemon juice and salt for 30 minutes. Dust with flour.
- **For the batter:** Mix all the ingredients (except oil) together in a bowl. Add approximately 4½ tbsp water and make a batter of coating consistency. Dip the chicken fingers in the batter. Heat the oil in a pan; deep-fry the chicken fingers until crisp and tender. Remove and drain on paper towels.
- Serve warm.

Presentation:

Place a ring (3″ diameter) and make a round bed of crisp spinach in the centre of a serving plate. Arrange 2 chicken fingers over the spinach bed and then place 3 more chicken fingers across. Pour the sour yoghurt sauce around. Divide the tomato concasse into 12 equal portions and arrange three portions on each plate. Sprinkle a little aromatic tangy masala over the tomato concasse.

entrées

Spiral Approach

Yield: 4 portions

A raw banana transformed into a gourmet kebab in a pastry spiral with date and raisin stuffing. A Bengal gram kebab in a tasty minty tomato sauce goes well with urad dal roti.

Ingredients:

For the banana kebabs:

Bananas, raw, peeled, mashed	7 oz/200 gm
Groundnut oil	1 tbsp
Ginger-garlic *(adrak-lasan)* paste	1 tsp
Green chillies, chopped	½ tsp
Ginger, chopped	½ tsp
Green coriander *(hara dhaniya)*, chopped	1 tbsp
Cornflour	2 tsp
White pepper *(safed mirch)* powder	½ tsp
Lemon *(nimbu)* juice	1 tsp
Cornflour to dust and oil for frying	
Dates *(khajoor)*, chopped	1 oz/28 gm
Mint and coriander sauce (see p.19)	2 tbsp

For the *ajwain* spiral:

Flaky pastry (see p.27)	4¼ oz/125 gm

For the dal kebabs:

Bengal gram *(chana dal)*	3½ oz/100 gm
Dry red chillies *(sookhi lal mirch)*	3
Green cardamoms *(choti elaichi)*	3
Cinnamon *(dalchini)* stick	1
Black peppercorns *(sabut kali mirch)*	15
Cumin *(jeera)* seeds	1 tsp
Cloves *(laung)*	8
Onions, chopped	3 tbsp
Ginger, chopped	1 tsp
Garlic, cloves	1 tsp
Salt to taste	
Cornflour for binding	1 tsp
Groundnut oil for deep-frying	

For the garnishing:

Mint and coriander sauce (see p.19)	4 tbsp
Tomato butter sauce (see p.16)	6 tbsp
Lemon, cut into wedges	4
Mint *(pudina)*	4 sprigs

Procedure:

- **For the banana kebabs:** Heat the oil; add ginger-garlic paste and bananas; cook till the mixture leaves the sides. Cool, add green chillies, ginger, green coriander, cornflour, salt, pepper, and lemon juice; mix. Divide the mixture into 4 equal portions. With greased hands, spread a portion on a 6″ long wooden stick by pressing along the length of the skewer to make 3½″ long kebab. Dust with cornflour. Repeat with the other portions.
- Heat the oil; deep-fry the kebabs along with the wooden stick until brown. Remove the stick gently. Slit the kebab lengthwise and stuff with a mixture of dates and mint and coriander sauce.
- **For the *ajwain* spiral:** Make a dough with one egg and follow the rest of the recipe on p.27. Roll the dough thin (1 mm) and cut into long strips with ¼″ width. Wrap the strips on a round pipe (¾″ diameter) covered with silver foil and make 4″ spirals. Bake in a moderately hot oven till golden brown. Gently remove the *ajwain* spirals and insert a banana kebab in it.
- **For the dal kebabs:** Mix all the ingredients (except oil) together. Add about 5 cups water and boil until the Bengal gram is cooked and dry. Put the mixture in a mincer twice to make a fine paste. Divide into 4 equal portions and shape each into a patty (1½″x½″). Heat the oil in a pan; deep-fry the patties until golden brown. Serve warm.

Presentation:

Pour 1 tbsp mint and coriander sauce on one side of the plate. Place the Bengal gram kebab over it. Pour the tomato butter sauce around the mint and coriander sauce and make a design as shown in the picture with the help of a toothpick. Place the *ajwain* spiral stuffed with banana kebab at an angle and garnish with lemon wedges and mint sprigs.

Studded Platter

Yield: 4 portions

Grilled cottage cheese, peppers, and tomatoes served with spinach patty in a thick tomato gravy accompanied with kali mirch gajar roti.

Ingredients:

For the spinach patties:

Spinach *(palak)* paste	2¾ oz/75 gm
Bengal gram *(chana dal)*	3½ oz/100 gm
Green cardamoms *(choti elaichi)*	3
Cinnamon *(dalchini)* stick	1
Cloves *(laung)*	3
Processed cheese, grated	1 tbsp
Butter	2 tbsp
Mace *(javitri)* powder	a pinch
Cumin *(jeera)* powder	a pinch
Fenugreek *(methi)* powder	a pinch
Yellow chilli powder	a pinch
Salt to taste	
Lemon *(nimbu)* juice	1½ tbsp
Groundnut oil for shallow frying	

For the saffron potatoes:

Potatoes, scooped, ½", cooked	12
Groundnut oil	1 tsp
Turmeric *(haldi)* powder	a pinch
Red chilli powder	a pinch
Salt to taste	
Saffron *(kesar)* sauce (see p.18)	8 tbsp

For the grilled vegetables:

Cottage cheese *(paneer)*, diced into 1"x¾"x1/8" squares	16
Red, yellow, green peppers, diced into 1"x¾"x1/8" squares	16
Tomatoes, diced into 1"x¾"x1/8" squares	16
Marinade for the vegetables (see p.64)	
Groundnut oil	1 tsp

For the garnishing:

Saffron *(kesar)* sauce	4 tbsp
Tomato butter sauce (see p.16)	8 tbsp
Crisp spinach (see p.13)	½ oz/14 gm
Lemon, cut into wedges	4
Mint *(pudina)*	4 sprigs

Procedure:

- **For the spinach patties:** Mix Bengal gram with green cardamoms, cinnamon stick, cloves, and about 5 cups water; boil until the Bengal gram is cooked and dry. Put it in a mincer twice and make a fine paste.
- Heat the butter in a pan; add spinach paste and sauté until dry. Add Bengal gram paste and sauté until the mixture leaves the sides. Remove, mix in the spices and salt. Divide into 4 portions and shape into patties. Grease a griddle *(tawa)* and fry both the sides over low heat until crisp and brown on the surface. Serve warm.
- **For the saffron potatoes:** Heat the oil; add the potatoes, turmeric powder, red chilli powder, and salt; mix well.
- Add the saffron sauce, bring to the boil and then simmer for 1-2 minutes. Adjust the sauce consistency.
- **For the grilled vegetables:** Marinate the vegetables and cottage cheese for 30 minutes. Remove and arrange the cottage cheese and peppers on a griller, sprinkle oil and grill to make criss-cross marks. Similarly, grill the tomatoes for a shorter period.

Presentation:

Pour 1 tbsp saffron sauce in the centre of the plate. Place a spinach patty over it. Pour the tomato butter sauce around the saffron sauce and arrange the grilled vegetables around it. Divide the crisp spinach into 4 portions and arrange a portion of it at the top periphery of the plate. Arrange 3 saffron potato balls over it. Garnish with lemon wedges and mint sprigs.

Gold Rush

Yield: 4 portions

Cottage cheese burnished with pure saffron, filled with tomato butter sauce and served with onion rings offset with a tomato chutney. A mutter kulcha *completes the dish.*

Ingredients:

Cottage cheese *(paneer)*, cut into 2"x2"x1" squares	4 (7 oz/200 gm)
For the marinade:	
Processed cheese, mashed	1¾ oz/50 gm
Ginger-garlic *(adrak-lasan)* paste	1 tsp
Hung yoghurt *(dahi)*	1 tbsp
Yellow chilli powder	½ tsp
Turmeric *(haldi)* powder	½ tsp
Fennel *(saunf)* powder	½ tsp
Green chilli paste	1 tsp
Salt to taste	
Cream	2 tbsp
Saffron *(kesar)*, soaked in 2 tsp warm water	½ gm
Tomato butter sauce (see p.16)	4 tbsp
For the garnishing:	
Tomato chutney (see p.19)	6 tbsp
Curry leaves *(kadhi patta)*, deep-fried	12
Tomato and lemon rosettes (see p.122)	4
Lemon, cut into wings (see p.124)	8
Onion rings, fried (see p.60)	12

Procedure:

- Scoop the cottage cheese squares in the middle (1" diameter and ¼" deep).
- **For the marinade:** Mix all the ingredients (except the tomato butter sauce) and rub into the cottage cheese squares. Keep aside for 30 minutes. Skewer the cottage cheese squares and roast in a moderately hot tandoor for 3-4 minutes or alternatively roast in a moderately hot oven for 5-7 minutes. Remove from the skewers.
- Heat the tomato butter sauce and fill in the middle of the cottage cheese squares.

Presentation:

Spread 1½ tbsp tomato chutney in the centre of the plate; arrange a cottage cheese square over it and decorate with 3 curry leaves on one side of the tomato chutney. Arrange a tomato and lemon rosette along with 2 lemon wings on the top periphery of the place. Place 3 fried onion rings on the bottom periphery of the plate.

Potato Premium

Yield: 4 portions

A tandoori stuffed potato, a skewer of cottage cheese and vegetables with mint chutney together with a tangy tamarind sauce goes well with moong dal roti.

Ingredients:

For the cottage cheese and vegetable kebabs:

Vegetables, boiled with turmeric powder, squeezed, roughly mashed	4 oz/120 gm
Potatoes, boiled, roughly mashed	2 oz/56 gm
Yellow chilli powder	½ tsp
Green chillies, finely chopped	½ tsp
Ginger *(adrak)*, finely chopped	½ tsp
Green coriander *(hara dhaniya)*, chopped	1 tsp
Gram flour *(besan)*, roasted	2 tsp
Breadcrumbs, fresh	2 tsp
Clove *(laung)* powder	a pinch
Cardamom *(elaichi)* powder	a pinch
Mace *(javitri)* powder	a pinch
Black pepper *(kali mirch)* powder	a pinch
Cottage cheese *(paneer)*, mashed	4 tbsp
Salt to taste	

For the tandoori potatoes:

Potatoes, cylindrical shape, scooped from the middle (1¾" diameter x 2½" length)	4 (7 oz/200 gm)
Potato trimmings, peeled	4 oz/120 gm
Groundnut oil for deep-frying	
Ginger, chopped	½ tsp
Green chillies, finely chopped	½ tsp
Mint *(pudina)*, chopped	1 tsp
Yellow chilli powder	½ tsp
Cashew nuts *(kaju)*, broken, fried	½ oz/14 gm
Raisins *(kishmish)*, deep-fried	½ oz/14 gm
Black pepper *(kali mirch)* powder	a pinch
Aromatic tangy masala (see p.12)	½ tsp
Salt to taste	
Black cumin *(shahi jeera)* powder	½ tsp
Lemon *(nimbu)* juice	1 tbsp

For the garnishing:

Sweet date and tamarind sauce (see p.18)	4 tbsp
Mint and coriander sauce (see p.19)	4 tbsp
Laccha salad (see p.58)	3 oz/80 gm
Lemon *(nimbu)*, cut into wedges	4
Mint *(pudina)*	4 sprigs

Procedure:

- **For the cottage cheese and vegetable kebabs:** Mix all the ingredients together and divide into 4 equal portions (Yield: 8½ oz/240 gm). With wet hands, spread a portion by pressing them along the length of the skewer, making the kebab 6" long. Roast in a moderately hot tandoor until golden brown in colour. Remove gently and trim the sides. Serve warm.
- **For the tandoori potatoes:** Heat the oil in a pan; deep-fry the potato cylinders along with the trimmings until the trimmings are golden brown and potato cylinders are ¾th cooked. Cool the trimmings and mash roughly. Mix this with the remaining ingredients and fill this mixture into the potato cylinders. Put the potatoes on a skewer and roast in the moderately hot tandoor until golden brown. Remove and cut into half, horizontally. Serve warm.

Presentation:

Pipe a paisley with sweet date and tamarind sauce and fill in with the mint and coriander sauce. Spread the salad in the centre of the plate and place the tandoori potato over it. Arrange the cottage cheese and vegetable kebab on the top periphery of the plate. Garnish with lemon wedges and mint sprigs.

Pancake Perfection

Yield: 4 portions

Gram flour pancake stuffed with cottage cheese and vegetable kebab, served with a refreshing salad, stuffed green chillies and piaz kali mirch roti.

Ingredients:

For the gram flour rolls:

Gram flour *(besan)*	2 oz/56 gm
Green coriander *(hara dhaniya)*, chopped	1 tbsp
Salt to taste	
Groundnut oil for shallow frying	
Cottage cheese *(paneer)* and vegetable kebabs (see p.53)	3

For the fried stuffed chillies:

Whole green chillies, slit	8
Potatoes, boiled, mashed	3 tbsp
Green coriander, chopped	1 tbsp
Aromatic garam masala (see p.12)	a pinch
Groundnut oil for deep-frying	

For the garnishing:

Laccha salad (see p.58)	4 portions
Tomato roses (see p.122)	4
Lemon *(nimbu)*, cut into wedges	4
Pastry bows (see p.29)	4
Mint and coriander sauce (see p.19)	4 tbsp

Procedure:

- **For the gram flour rolls:** Mix gram flour with green coriander, salt and approximately ¾ cup water and make a smooth batter of pouring consistency. Divide into 3 equal portions.
- Heat some oil in a non-stick pan; pour a portion of the batter and make a 7″ diameter pancake. Remove. Roll the cottage cheese and vegetable kebab in the pancake, trim the sides and cut the roll into half (i.e. 6 pieces in all) and then each portion into 2 diagonally.
- **For the fried stuffed chillies:** Mix the potatoes with green coriander and aromatic garam masala and fill in the slit chillies. Heat the oil; deep-fry the chillies for 30 seconds. Remove and drain.

Presentation:

Arrange 3 pieces of cut gram flour rolls in the centre of the plate. Place a portion of the salad on one side. Arrange a tomato rose and two fried green chillies on top of the plate. Arrange one pastry bow at the bottom. Pour 1 tbsp mint and coriander sauce near the gram flour rolls.

Triple Decker

Yield: 4 portions

Steamed Bengal gram cake with tangy tomato chutney, fresh salad and tasty fried chillies accompanied with missi roti.

Ingredients:

Bengal gram *(chana dal)*	8½ oz/240 gm
Ginger *(adrak)* paste	1 tsp
Green chilli paste	½ tsp
Salt to taste	
Soda bicarbonate	½ tsp
Sugar	1 tsp

For the tempering:

Sugar	3 tbsp
Green chillies, slit, deseeded	4
Groundnut oil	1½ tbsp
Mustard seeds *(rai)*	1 tsp
Lemon *(nimbu)* juice	4 tsp

For the garnishing:

Tomato chutney (see p.19)	8 tbsp
Mint coriander sauce (see p.19)	8 tbsp
Stuffed green chillies (see p.55)	4
Laccha salad (see p.58)	3 oz/80 gm

Procedure:

- Soak Bengal gram in water for 3-4 hours and drain. Put the dal in a grinder, add approximately ½ cup water and make a smooth paste. Remove and keep overnight in a warm place to ferment. Beat the dal paste to a fluffy consistency. Add ginger paste, green chilli paste, salt, soda bicarbonate (dissolved in 1 tsp water), and sugar; mix well.
- Spread the mixture in a well-oiled tray (10″x5″x3″) and steam for 15-18 minutes or till cooked. (To check if done, pierce a knife and see that the knife comes out clean). Remove and cool.
- **For the tempering:** Dissolve the sugar in approximately ¾ cup water. Add green chillies. Heat the oil in a pan; add mustard seeds and when they crackle put the sugar-chilli mixture and cook for 3-4 minutes. Add lemon juice, stir. Pour the tempering over the cake and chill.
- Demould and cut the steamed cake into slices (4″x3″x1″ thick). Spread the tomato chutney on one slice and mint coriander sauce on the other. Put tomato chutney slice over the mint coriander slice and cover with a plain gram flour slice. Cut the sandwiched gram flour cake into 1″ slices.

Presentation:

Spread 1 tbsp tomato chutney in the top periphery and a spoonful of mint and coriander sauce at the bottom of the serving plate. Place the gram flour slice in the centre. Arrange the stuffed fried chilli and the salad on either side of the gram flour cake.

Double Edge

Yield: 4 portions

A twin combination seekh kebab with lamb mince enclosed in delicious chicken mince accompanied by tangy tomato chutney and fresh salad. Urad dal roti *adds to the taste.*

Ingredients:

For the lamb mince: (Yield: 10½ oz)	
Lamb, boneless, 1″ chunks	8½ oz/240 gm
Ginger *(adrak)*, chopped	2 tsp
Garlic *(lasan)*, chopped	1 tbsp
Green chilli	1
Lamb fat	1¾ oz/50 gm
For the lamb *seekh* kebab:	
Lamb mince (from above)	10½ oz/300 gm
Ginger-garlic paste	1 tsp
Ginger, finely chopped	½ tsp
Green chillies, finely chopped	½ tsp
Green coriander *(hara dhaniya)*, chopped	1 tbsp
Mace-cardamom *(javitri-elaichi)* powder	½ tsp
Red chilli paste	1 tsp
Groundnut oil	1 tsp
Lemon *(nimbu)* juice	2 tsp
For chicken mince: (Yield: 9 oz)	
Chicken, boneless chunks	9 oz/250 gm
Ginger, chopped	1 tsp
Garlic, chopped	1 tsp
Green chilli	1
Lamb fat	½ oz/14 gm
For the chicken kebab:	
Chicken mince (from above)	9 oz/250 gm
Ginger, finely chopped	1 tsp
White pepper *(safed mirch)*	½ tsp
Green coriander, chopped	1 tbsp
Mace-cardamom powder	½ tsp
Bread, soaked in milk, squeezed	½ oz/14 gm
Cashew nut *(kaju)* paste	1½ tbsp
Salt to taste	
For the *laccha* salad:	
Carrots *(gajar)*, cut into thin spirals	1½ oz/40 gm
Cucumbers *(khira)*, cut into spirals	1½ oz/40 gm
Tomato, julienned	¾ oz/20 gm
Red cabbage, julienned	2 tbsp
Black peppercorns, *(sabut kali mirch)*, crushed	a pinch
Cumin yoghurt sauce (see p.19)	1 tbsp
For the garnishing:	
Tomato chutney (see p.19)	12 tbsp
Lemon stars	4
Mint *(pudina)*	4 sprigs
Curry leaves *(kadhi patta)*, fried	12

Procedure:

- **For the lamb mince:** Put all the ingredients in a mincer thrice and make a fine and soft mince.
- **For the lamb *seekh* kebab:** Knead all the ingredients together. Divide into 4 equal portions. With wet hands, spread a portion by pressing along the length of the skewer (6″ long). Roast in a moderately hot tandoor for 6-7 minutes. Remove and hang the skewer for 4-5 minutes to allow the excess moisture to drip off. Cool (do not remove from the skewer).
- **For the chicken mince:** Put all the ingredients in a mincer twice and make a fine and soft mince.
- **For the chicken kebab:** Knead all the ingredients together; chill. Divide into 4 equal portions. With wet hands, spread a portion over the cooked *seekh* kebab by pressing along the length of the skewer. Roast in a moderately hot tandoor for 3-4 minutes. Remove and hang the skewer for 4-5 minutes. Roast again in the tandoor for 2 minutes. Remove the kebab gently and trim the sides. Cut into 1½″ pieces.
- **For the *laccha* salad:** Mix all the ingredients gently together. Divide into 4 equal portions. Put a portion in a mould (2″ diameter x ½″ height). Press gently and remove the mould. This will help in retaining the shape of the salad.

Presentation:

Spread 3 tbsp tomato chutney on the top periphery of the plate. Arrange 3 pieces of chicken and lamb kebab on top. Place a portion of the salad, lemon star, mint sprig, and fried curry leaves as shown in the picture.

Hidden Treasure

Yield: 4 portions

Succulent morsels of barbequed chicken in a pastry cage. Lamb mince enclosed in a quail egg served with kali mirch gajar roti.

Ingredients:

For the first chicken marinade:
Chicken thighs, skinless, with bone 4 (10½ oz/300 gm)
Lemon *(nimbu)* juice 1½ tbsp
Ginger-garlic *(adrak-lasan)* paste 4 tsp
Salt to taste

For the second marinade:
Yoghurt *(dahi)*, hung 5¼ oz/150 gm
Lemon juice 1½ tbsp
Ginger-garlic paste 4 tsp
Red chilli paste 2 tsp
Mace-cardamom *(javitri-elaichi)* powder ½ tsp
Clove *(laung)* powder ½ tsp
Groundnut oil 4 tsp
Salt to taste
Red colour 2 tsp

For the quail eggs:
Quail eggs, hard-boiled 2
Lamb mince (see p.58) 2 oz/56 gm
Groundnut oil for deep-frying

For the fried onion rings:
Onions, cut into rings, 1½" diameter 1½ oz/40 gm
Cornflour 5 tsp
Flour *(maida)* 4 tsp
Baking powder ½ tsp
Ginger-garlic paste ½ tsp
Carom seeds *(ajwain)* a pinch
Red chilli powder a pinch
Salt to taste
Flour for dusting
Groundnut oil for deep-frying
Aromatic tangy masala (see p.12) to sprinkle

For the *ajwain* cage:
(Yield: 12 cages)
Flour 3¼ cups
Ghee 7 tbsp
Salt to taste
Carom seeds 4 tsp
Water ¾ cup
Egg wash
Groundnut oil for frying

For the garnishing:
Mint and coriander sauce (see p.19) 8 tbsp
Green coriander *(hara dhaniya)* 4 sprigs
Lemon *(nimbu)*, cut into wedges 4

Procedure:

- **For the first marinade:** Rub the lemon juice, ginger-garlic paste, and salt over the chicken and keep aside for 15 minutes. Drain the excess marinade and transfer chicken to the second marinade.
- **For the second marinade:** Mix all the ingredients together. Marinate the chicken thighs for 2 hours. Remove the chicken thighs from the marinade, skewer and roast in a moderately hot tandoor for 10-12 minutes. Remove, hang the skewers for 4-5 minutes to allow the excess moisture to drip off. Baste with butter, remove the bones gently and roast in the tandoor again for 1-2 minutes.
- **For the quail eggs:** Cover the eggs with the mince and shape like an egg. Heat the oil and deep-fry the eggs until the lamb is cooked. Remove and cut into half.
- **For the fried onion rings:** Mix all the ingredients together (except onion rings, flour for dusting, oil, and tangy masala). Add approximately ¼ cup water and make a thick batter. Keep the batter aside for 15 minutes. Dust the onion rings with flour, dip in the batter and deep-fry. Sprinkle little aromatic tangy masala before serving.
- **For the *ajwain* cage:** Melt the ghee and add to the flour; mix till it resembles breadcrumbs. Add salt, carom seeds, and water and knead to make a hard dough. Cover the dough with a wet cloth for about 30 minutes. Roll into a rectangular shape (2 mm thick). Cut strips of 8 mm width and apply an egg wash. Arrange the strips leaving gaps in between (lengthwise). Arrange the other strips overlapping the alternate strips resembling a mat, with an even gap in between.

- Cut the mat with a 5″ diameter cutter. Place each mat on the greased mould (3″ diameter x 1½″ height). Shape the cage by pressing the edges towards the mould. Bake at 200°C/400°F for about 5 minutes along with the mould. Remove the cage gently from the mould. Heat the oil and deep-fry the cage gently until golden brown.

Presentation:

Spread 2 tbsp of mint and coriander sauce on the top of the plate. Place the barbecued chicken and cover it with the *ajwain* cage. Arrange 3 fried onion rings at the bottom of the plate and place a half cut quail egg in the centre ring. Decorate with green coriander and lemon wedge. (See photograph on p.44)

Sea Splendour

Yield: 4 portions

A shallow fried turmeric and chilli pomfret goes well with a mildly spiced lamb kebab with two delicious sauces. To be savoured with pudina mutter roti.

Ingredients:

Pomfret fillets	4 (2 oz/56 gm)
Turmeric *(haldi)* powder	1 tsp
Red chilli powder	1 tsp
Lemon *(nimbu)* juice	1½ tbsp
Salt to taste	
Flour *(maida)* to dust fillets	
Groundnut oil for shallow frying	
For the lamb kebab:	
Lamb mince (see p.58)	10½ oz/300 gm
For the garnishing:	
Tomato butter sauce (see p.16)	8 tbsp
Sour yoghurt sauce (see p.16)	12 tbsp
Lemon stars	4
Mint *(pudina)*	4 sprigs

Procedure:

- Rub turmeric powder, red chilli powder, lemon juice, and salt on the fish fillets. Dust the fillets with flour and shallow fry on both sides until cooked.
- **For the lamb kebab:** Divide the mixture into 4 portions. With wet hand, spread a portion by pressing along the length of the skewer making each kebab 7″ long. Roast in a moderately hot tandoor for 6-7 minutes. Remove and hang the skewer for 4-5 minutes to allow the excess moisture to drip off. Roast again for 2 minutes. Remove the kebab gently, trim the sides and cut into 3″ pieces. Serve warm.

Presentation:

Place the turmeric chilli pomfret as shown in the picture. Pour 2 tbsp of tomato butter sauce around the fish. Now pour 3 tbsp of sour yoghurt sauce around the tomato butter sauce. Arrange 2 lamb kebabs on either side of the plate and a lemon star and mint sprig on the top.

Magnificent Duo

Yield: 4 portions

Chicken shashlik and marinated prawn masala with a tossed salad and mint dressing, tastes perfect with a moong dal roti.

Ingredients:

For the chicken shashlik:

Chicken kebab mince (see p.58)	7 oz/200 gm
Onions, diced into 1″x1″ pieces	16
Capsicums *(Shimla mirch)*, diced into 1″x1″ pieces	16
Tomatoes, diced into 1″x1″ pieces	16
Groundnut oil	1 tsp

Marinade for the vegetables:

Groundnut oil	4 tbsp
White vinegar *(sirka)*	2 tsp
Sugar	a pinch
Aromatic garam masala (see p.12)	a pinch
Cumin *(jeera)* powder	a pinch
Black cumin *(shahi jeera)* powder	a pinch
Red chilli powder	a pinch
Salt to taste	

For the chilli prawns:

Prawns, large, peeled with tail on	4
Turmeric *(haldi)* powder	1 tsp
Red chilli powder	a pinch
Salt to taste	
Lemon *(nimbu)* juice	2 tsp
Groundnut oil	3½ tbsp

For the garnishing:

Lemon, cut into wings (see p.124)	4
Mint *(pudina)*	4 sprigs
Laccha salad (see p.58)	4 portions
Tomato butter sauce with crisp spinach (see p.16)	4 tbsp

Procedure:

- **For the chicken shashlik:** Divide the chicken kebab mince into 4 equal portions. With a wet hand, spread a portion pressing along the length of the skewer, making the kebab 5″ long. Roast in a moderately hot tandoor for 4-5 minutes. Remove and hang the skewer for 4-5 minutes to allow the excess moisture to drip off. Remove gently, trim the sides and cut the kebab into 4 equal sizes (1″ approximately).
- **For the marinade:** Mix all the ingredients together. Marinate the vegetables for 30 minutes. Remove. Skewer each variety of vegetable and the cut chicken kebab. Heat a well-oiled griddle plate; place the skewered shashlik and sauté over medium heat turning occasionally until the vegetables are well roasted.
- **For the chilli prawns:** Shape the prawn like a butterfly. Take out the tail from below the prawn through the centre. Wrap the tail with a silver foil. Marinate the prawns with turmeric powder, red chilli powder, salt, and lemon juice for 30 minutes.
- Heat the oil in a pan; add the prawns and place the pan in a moderately hot oven for 3 minutes or until cooked. Remove the prawns from the pan, discard the silver foil and clean the tail.
- Serve warm.

Presentation:

Remove the shashlik from the skewer and place at an angle on one side of the plate. Pour 1 tbsp of tomato butter sauce with crisp spinach on the other side and place a chilli prawn on it. Arrange the *laccha* salad mould, lemon wing, and mint sprig at the bottom of the plate.

Match Mate

Yield: 4 portions

Barbequed chicken mosaique with a tasty shrimp roll combines well with mint chutney, sour yoghurt sauce and a piaz kali mirch roti.

Ingredients:

For the first chicken marinade:

Chicken thighs, skinless with bone	4 (10½ oz/300 gm)
Lemon *(nimbu)* juice	4 tsp
Ginger-garlic *(adrak-lasan)* paste	4 tsp
Salt to taste	

For the second chicken marinade:

Processed cheese, finely grated	5 tbsp
Cream	½ cup
Egg	1
Cornflour	2 tsp
Green coriander *(hara dhaniya)*, chopped	1 tbsp
Mace *(javitri)* powder	a pinch
Cardamom *(elaichi)* powder	a pinch
Salt to taste	

For the prawn rolls:

Prawn mince	8 oz/225 gm
Ginger-garlic paste	2 tsp
Ginger, finely chopped	1 tsp
Green chillies, finely chopped	½ tsp
Green coriander, finely chopped	1 tbsp
Mace powder	a pinch
Cardamom powder	a pinch
Egg	1
Groundnut oil	1 tsp
Salt to taste	

For the crunchy salad:

Red cabbage, diced	1½ oz/40 gm
Tomatoes, diced into ½"x½" pieces	2 oz/56 gm
Cucumbers *(khira)*, deseeded, diced into ½"x½"	2 oz/56 gm
Cabbage *(bandh gobi)*, diced	1½ oz/40 gm
Lemon juice	2 tsp
Salt and black pepper to taste	
Aromatic tangy masala (see p.12)	a pinch

For the garnishing:

Lemon, cut into wedges	4
Mint *(pudina)*	4 sprigs
Sour yoghurt sauce (see p.16)	4 tbsp
Mint and coriander sauce (see p.19)	4 tsp

Procedure:

- **For the first chicken marinade:** Rub all the ingredients on the chicken and keep aside for 15 minutes. Remove and squeeze.
- **For the second chicken marinade:** Mix the cheese, cream, and egg into a smooth mixture. Add the remaining ingredients and mix. Soak the chicken thighs in the marinade for 2 hours.
- Remove the chicken from the marinade, skewer and roast in a moderately hot tandoor for 8-9 minutes. Remove, hang the skewer for 4-5 minutes to allow the excess moisture to drip off. Remove the bone gently. Make criss-cross marks on the chicken with a red hot rod. Re-skewer and roast in the tandoor for 1-2 minutes. Serve warm.
- **For the prawn rolls:** Mix all the ingredients together and knead well. Divide into 4 equal portions. With a wet hand spread a portion by pressing along the length of the skewer, making each kebab 7" long. Roast in a moderately hot tandoor for 4-5 minutes. Remove, hang the skewer for 4-5 minutes to allow the excess moisture to drip off. Roast again for 1-2 minutes. Remove from the skewer gently. Serve warm.
- **For the crunchy salad:** Mix all the ingredients together and divide into 4 equal portions.

Presentation:

Spread a portion of the tangy crunchy salad on the bottom periphery of the plate and place the chicken on top. Cut the prawn roll slantwise and arrange on the top periphery of the plate. Pour 1 tbsp sour yoghurt on one side and 1 tsp coriander and mint sauce over it. Place a lemon wedge and mint sprig.

Drum Beat

Yield: 4 portions

Barbequed stuffed chicken drumstick with spiced vegetables. A spiral fish roll with mint chutney accompanied with missi roti.

Ingredients:

For the fish rolls:

Bekti fillets, cut into 4 strips (12″x ½″x¼″)	4 (10½ oz/300 gm)
Lemon *(nimbu)* juice	4 tsp
Salt to taste	
Mint and coriander sauce (see p.19)	1 cup
Groundnut oil	2 tsp
Gram flour *(besan)*	6 tbsp
Carom seeds *(ajwain)*	a pinch
Groundnut oil to sauté	

For the pickled chicken:

Chicken drumsticks, boneless	4 (7¾ oz/220 gm)
Ginger-garlic *(adrak-lasan)* paste	1 tbsp
Lemon juice	1 tbsp
Salt to taste	
Chicken mince (see p.58)	2¾ oz/75 gm
Mixed mango pickle, chopped	1 tsp
Cheese marinade (see p.66)	¾ cup

For the spiced vegetables:

Carrots *(gajar)*, scooped, blanched	12
Potatoes, scooped, blanched	8
Groundnut oil	1 tsp
Turmeric *(haldi)* powder	a pinch
Red chilli powder	a pinch
Salt to taste	
Lemon juice	1 tsp

For the crunchy salad:

Tomatoes, diced into ½″x½″ pieces	2 oz/56 gm
Cucumbers *(khira)*, diced into ½″x½″ pieces	2 oz/56 gm
Cabbage *(bandh gobi)*, diced into coarsely pieces	1½ oz/40 gm
Red cabbage *(lal gobi)*, diced into ½″x½″ pieces	1½ oz/40 gm
Lemon juice	2 tsp
Salt and black pepper to taste	
Aromatic tangy masala (see p.12)	a pinch

For the garnishing:

Lemon, cut into wedges	4
Mint *(pudina)* / Green coriander *(hara dhaniya)*	4 sprigs

Procedure:

- **For the fish rolls:** Marinate the fish strips with lemon juice and salt for 15 minutes. Then rub mint and coriander sauce and oil. Keep aside for 30 minutes. Roll the strips into spirals and secure together with toothpicks. Marinate the fish rolls in the sauce mixture for 15 minutes and refrigerate. Remove, dust with gram flour, carom seeds and salt mixture. Heat the oil on a griddle; sauté the fish spiral rolls on both sides for 8-10 minutes or until cooked. Remove the toothpicks. Serve warm.
- **For the pickled chicken:** Rub ginger-garlic paste, lemon juice, and salt on the chicken drumsticks and keep aside for 15 minutes. Squeeze. Mix the chicken mince and mango pickle together and fill in the drumsticks. Marinate the chicken in the cheese marinade for 15 minutes. Now wrap the drumsticks tightly with silver foil; skewer and roast in a moderately hot tandoor for 10 minutes. Cool, remove the foil, hang the skewer for 4-5 minutes to allow the excess moisture to drip off. Roast in a tandoor for another 4-5 minutes.
- **For the spiced vegetables:** Heat the oil in a pan; add the spices, vegetables, and salt; toss for 2-3 minutes. Sprinkle lemon juice and remove.
- **For the crunchy salad:** Mix all the ingredients together and divide into 4 equal portions.

Presentation:

Place a fish roll in the centre of the plate and arrange carrot and potatoes scoops alternatively around the fish roll. Place the pickled drumstick on one side on the plate. Spread the salad on the top periphery of the plate. Arrange a lemon wedge and mint sprig on the salad.

main course

Gracious Accord

Yield: 4 portions

Spicy cottage cheese, roasted cauliflower florets and crisp okra served with green pea pulao and aubergine quenelles. Creamy dal goes well with roomali roti.

Ingredients:

For the spicy cottage cheese:

Cottage cheese, diced into ¼″ pieces	7oz/200 gm
Ghee	4 tsp
Onions, diced into ½″ pieces	1½ oz/40 gm
Turmeric *(haldi)* powder	1 tsp
Cumin *(jeera)* powder	½ tsp
Tomatoes, diced into ½″ pieces	2 oz/56 gm
Green chillies, chopped	1 tsp
Cream	5 tsp
Green coriander *(hara dhaniya)*, chopped	1 tbsp
Aromatic tangy masala (see p.12)	½ tsp
Lemon *(nimbu)* juice	1 tsp
Salt to taste	

For the roasted cauliflower:

Cauliflower *(phool gobi)*, cut into 4 florets, blanched with turmeric and salt	3½ oz/100 gm
Lemon juice	1 tsp
Red chilli powder	a pinch
Aromatic tangy masala (see p.12)	a pinch
Gram flour *(besan)*	5 tsp
Ginger-garlic *(adrak-lasan)* paste	½ tsp
Red chilli powder	a pinch
Black peppercorns *(sabut kali mirch)*, crushed	½ tsp
Lemon juice	1 tsp
Salt to taste	
Groundnut oil for deep-frying	
Tomato butter sauce (see p.16)	4 tbsp

For the pine nut and spinach pulao:

Pulao (see p.106)	11 oz/320 gm
Crisp spinach (see p.13)	½ oz/14 gm
Pine nuts, roasted	1½ oz/40 gm

Creamy dal (see p.107)	8 tbsp
Spicy aubergine quenelles (see p.85)	8
Crisp okra (see p.92)	3 oz/80 gm

Procedure:

- **For the spicy cottage cheese:** Heat the ghee in a pan; add onions and sauté until golden brown. Add turmeric powder and cumin powder; mix well. Add tomatoes, green chillies, cottage cheese, and cream; stir for 1-2 minutes. Add green coriander, aromatic tangy masala, lemon juice, and salt; stir. Divide into 4 equal portions.
- **For the roasted cauliflower:** Sprinkle lemon juice, red chilli powder, and aromatic tangy masala on the cauliflower. Make a batter with gram flour, approximately 2½ tbsp water and the remaining ingredients. Dip the florets in the batter and deep-fry in hot oil until golden brown. Serve warm.
- **For the pine nut and spinach pulao:** Mix the pulao with the nut and spinach. Divide into 4 equal portions and fill in the moulds. Steam for a minute and demould each on the plate.

Presentation:

Make a round base of the spicy cottage cheese in the centre of the serving plate with the help of a ring (3″ diameter) and arrange the rice mould on top. Pour 1 tbsp of tomato butter sauce on the top periphery of the plate and place a cauliflower floret over it. Pour 2 tbsp of creamy dal on the bottom periphery of the plate. Arrange 2 spicy aubergine quenelles on one side and crisp okra on the other side.

Aromatic Adventure

Yield: 4 portions

Cottage cheese spiced with a herbed tomato sauce served with potato scoops in a delicious saffron gravy, spinach mould and carrot flowers flavoured with cumin. Tomato pulao and badami naan *goes well with the dish.*

Ingredients:

For the cottage cheese in herbed tomato sauce:

Cottage cheese *(paneer)*, cut into 2¼"x½"x½" pieces	16/5¼ oz/150 gm
Tomato butter sauce (see p.16)	16 tbsp
Crisp spinach (see p.13)	½ oz/14 gm
Mace *(javitri)* powder	a pinch
Cardamom *(elaichi)* powder	a pinch
Fennel *(saunf)* powder	a pinch

For spicy carrot flowers:

Carrot flowers (see p.123), 24 pieces, blanched	3½ oz/100 gm
Ghee	1 tsp
Turmeric *(haldi)* powder	a pinch
Red chilli powder	a pinch
Cumin *(jeera)* powder	a pinch
Lemon *(nimbu)* juice	1 tsp
Salt to taste	

For potato balls in saffron sauce:

Potato balls, ¾" balls, cooked	12/4 oz/120 gm
Saffron sauce (see p.18)	16 tbsp
Fennel powder	a pinch
Cardamom *(elaichi)* powder	a pinch

For spinach moulds with dal:

Black gram *(urad dal)*, cooked dry	6¼ oz/175 gm
Ghee	2 tsp
Onions, chopped	2 tsp
Ginger *(adrak)*, chopped	½ tsp
Green chillies, chopped	½ tsp
Red chilli powder	a pinch
Tomatoes, chopped	5 tsp
Cumin powder	a pinch
Lemon juice	1 tsp
Salt to taste	
Mango powder *(amchur)*	a pinch
Green coriander *(hara dhaniya)*, chopped	1 tbsp
Spinach *(palak)* blanched	3 oz/80 gm

Pulao (see p.106)	12 oz/350 gm
Tomato concasse	1½ oz/40 gm

Procedure:

- **For the cottage cheese in herbed tomato sauce:** Heat the tomato butter sauce in a pan; add cottage cheese and bring to the boil. Add the remaining ingredients and stir gently. Adjust the sauce consistency. Remove.
- **For spicy carrot flowers:** Heat the ghee in a pan; add turmeric powder and chilli powder; stir over low heat. Add carrots and stir for a minute. Add cumin powder, lemon juice, and salt; sauté.
- **For potato balls in saffron sauce:** Heat the saffron sauce; add potatoes and bring to the boil. Add fennel and cardamom powders and stir. Adjust the sauce consistency.
- **For spinach moulds with dal:** Heat the ghee; add onion and sauté until golden brown. Add ginger, green chillies, and red chilli powder; sauté. Add tomato and cook for a minute. Add black gram and stir. Add cumin powder, lemon juice, salt, mango powder, and green coriander; stir well. Grease the mould (2" diameter x 1" height) and line with spinach leaves. Fill the mould with black gram; steam for 1 minute. Demould.
- Mix the pulao with tomato concasse. Divide into 8 equal portions and fill in the small moulds. Steam for a minute and demould two portions on each serving plate.

Presentation:

Place a spinach mould on the top periphery of the plate and arrange 3 carrot flowers on either side of the spinach mould. Arrange 4 cottage cheese pieces as shown in the photograph. Place 2 tomato pulao moulds on the sides. Arrange 3 potato scoops on the bottom periphery of the plate and pour saffron sauce on top.

Golden Glory

Yield: 4 portions

Cottage cheese and carrot balls in saffron sauce with stuffed tomato cup and spinach mould. Tasty brown rice, rich creamy dal, and layered missi roti *completes the spread.*

Ingredients:

For cottage cheese and carrot balls:

Cottage cheese *(paneer)* cut into ¾" pieces 12/4 oz/120 gm
Carrots *(gajar)*, cut into ¾" pieces, boiled 8/3 oz/80 gm
Saffron sauce (see p.18) 16 tbsp
Fennel *(saunf)* powder a pinch
Cardamom *(elaichi)* powder a pinch
Salt to taste

For the tomato cups:

Tomato cups, medium-sized, blanched, de-skinned 4/3½ oz/100 gm
Ghee 2 tsp
Onion, chopped 1 tbsp
Ginger, chopped ½ tsp
Green chillies, chopped ½ tsp
Red chilli powder a pinch
Turmeric *(haldi)* powder ½ tsp
Tomatoes, chopped 5 tsp
Potatoes, cut into ¼" cubes, boiled 3½ oz/100 gm
Green coriander *(hara dhaniya)*, chopped ½ tbsp
Aromatic tangy masala (see p.12) ½ tsp
Salt to taste

For the spinach mould with vegetables:

Vegetables, diced, blanched 7 oz/200 gm
Ghee 2 tsp
Onion, diced 1 tbsp
Ginger, chopped ½ tsp
Green chillies, chopped ½ tsp
Turmeric powder a pinch
Tomato, chopped 2 tbsp
Cumin *(jeera)* powder a pinch
Green coriander, chopped ½ tsp
Salt to taste
Cashew/*Shahi* sauce (see p.17) 4 tbsp
Spinach *(palak)*, blanched 3 oz/80 gm

Brown rice (see p.106) 12 oz/350 gm
Creamy dal (see p.107) 8 tbsp
Tomato butter sauce (see p.16) 8 tbsp

Procedure:

- **For cottage cheese and carrot balls:** Heat the saffron sauce; add cottage cheese and carrot balls; bring to the boil. Add fennel and cardamom powders; stir well. Adjust the sauce consistency.
- **For the tomato cups:** Heat the ghee; sauté the onion over medium heat until light brown. Add ginger, green chillies, red chilli powder, and turmeric powder; stir well. Add tomatoes and cook for 1-2 minutes. Add potatoes and stir for a minute. Add the remaining ingredients and mix. Divide the mixture into 4 equal portions. Fill each tomato cup with a portion of the mixture. Heat the cups for 30 seconds in a moderately hot oven.
- **For the spinach mould with vegetables:** Heat the ghee; sauté onion over medium heat until golden brown. Add ginger, green chillies, and turmeric powder; stir well. Add tomato and stir for a minute. Add the vegetables and continue stirring for 1-2 minutes. Add cumin powder, green coriander, cashew sauce, and salt; stir. Divide into 4 portions. Grease the moulds, line with spinach leaves and fill with a portion of the vegetables. Cover with foil, steam for a minute and demould.
- **For the brown rice:** Divide the rice into 4 equal portions and fill in the moulds. Steam for a minute and demould.

Presentation:

Place a mould of brown rice in the centre of the plate. Arrange 3 balls of cottage cheese and 2 scoops of carrots alternately and cover with saffron sauce. Pour 2 tbsp of creamy dal at the bottom periphery and the tomato butter sauce around the dal. Place a tomato cup and spinach mould on either side of the rice mould.

Variety Wonder

Yield: 4 portions

Spicy aubergines flavoured with yoghurt and tomato chutney served with tandoori stuffed potato on mint gravy, masala dal, and crisp okra. Moulds of tomato, saffron, and pine nut spinach pulao and cheese kulcha *add taste to the dish.*

Ingredients:

For the spicy aubergines:

- Aubergines *(baingan)*, long, cut into 1¼″ diameter x ¼″ thick roundels — 12/4 oz/120 gm
- Turmeric *(haldi)* powder — ½ tsp
- Red chilli powder — a pinch
- Cumin *(jeera)* powder — a pinch
- Salt to taste
- Groundnut oil for shallow frying
- Yoghurt *(dahi)*, hung — 4 tbsp
- Aromatic tangy masala (see p.12) — a pinch
- Salt to taste
- Tomato chutney (see p.19) — 4 tbsp

For the rice:

- Tomato pulao (see p.75) — 4 oz/120 gm
- Pine nut and spinach pulao (see p.73) — 4 oz/120 gm
- Saffron pulao (see p.106) — 4 oz/120 gm
- Spicy potatoes (see p.85)
- Masala dal (see p.107) — 6 tbsp
- Mint and coriander sauce (see p.19) — 4 tbsp
- Tandoori stuffed potatoes, sliced (see p.53) — 4
- Tomato butter sauce (see p.16) — 4 tbsp
- Crisp okra (see p.92) — 3 oz/80 gm

Procedure:

- **For the spicy aubergines:** Coat the aubergines with turmeric powder, red chilli powder, cumin powder, and salt. Heat the oil in a pan; shallow fry the aubergines on both sides.
- Mix aromatic tangy masala and salt with the hung yoghurt and divide the hung yoghurt and tomato chutney each into 12 equal portions. Spread yoghurt and then tomato chutney on the aubergine slices. Serve warm.
- **For the rice:** Divide each pulao into 4 equal portions and fill in the small moulds. Steam for half a minute and demould each on serving plates.
- Follow the pulao recipe and use a pinch of saffron in the vegetable stock.

Presentation:

Pipe the spicy potato mixture as shown in the photograph and fill the space in between with masala dal. Arrange 3 aubergine slices near the piped potato. Pour 1 tbsp mint and coriander sauce on one side and place a slice of stuffed tandoori potato on top. Arrange the crisp okra on the opposite side and place the 3 pulaos at the bottom periphery of the plate.

Delicious Delight

Yield: 4 portions

Mouth-watering koftas in buttery tomato sauce with crisp spinach and carrot buds. Chick pea biryani, creamy dal, and mutter kulcha *complement the dish.*

Ingredients:

For the koftas:

Cottage cheese *(paneer)*, mashed	2 oz/56 gm
Saffron *(kesar)* water	2 tsp
Salt to taste	
Vegetables, boiled, brunoise	4 oz/120 gm
Potatoes, mashed	2 oz/56 gm
Ginger *(adrak)*, chopped	½ tsp
Green chillies, chopped	½ tsp
Cumin *(jeera)* powder	½ tsp
Green coriander *(hara dhaniya)*, chopped	1 tbsp
Cornflour	2 tsp
Salt to taste and cornflour to dust	
Groundnut oil for deep-frying	
Tomato butter sauce (see p.16)	8 tbsp
Cardamom *(elaichi)* powder	a pinch
Fennel *(saunf)* powder	a pinch

For the crisp spinach:

Spinach *(palak)*	4/½ oz/14 gm
Red chilli powder	a pinch
Aromatic tangy masala (see p.12)	a pinch
Gram flour *(besan)*	2½ tbsp
Ginger-garlic *(adrak-lasan)* paste	½ tsp
Red chilli powder	a pinch
Lemon *(nimbu)* juice	1 tsp
Salt to taste	
Ground oil for frying	

For the carrot buds:

Carrot buds, blanched (see p.124)	16/2¼ oz/60 gm
Red chilli powder	a pinch
Cumin powder	a pinch
Lemon juice	1 tsp
Saffron sauce (see p.18)	4 tbsp
Salt to taste	

Chick pea biryani (see p.105)	11 oz/320 gm
Creamy dal (see p.107)	16 tbsp
Saffron sauce	16 tbsp

Procedure:

- **For the koftas:** Mix cottage cheese with saffron water and salt; divide into 6 equal portions and shape into balls. Mix the vegetables with remaining ingredients and divide into 6 equal portions. Spread a portion and place a cottage cheese ball in the middle of the vegetable mixture; shape into a ball. Dust with cornflour and deep-fry until golden. Remove, cut each kofta into half. Heat the tomato butter sauce; add cardamom and fennel powders; stir well. Adjust the souce consistency.
- **For the crisp spinach:** Sprinkle red chilli powder and aromatic tangy masala on the wet spinach leaves. Make a batter of coating consistency with gram flour, approximately 4 tbsp water, and the remaining ingredients. Dip the spinach leaves in the batter and then deep-fry until golden brown and crisp.
- **For the carrot buds:** Heat saffron sauce; add red chilli powder, cumin powder, lemon juice, carrot buds, and salt; stir for 1 minute.
- Divide the chick pea biryani into 4 portions and fill in the moulds. Steam for a minute and demould each on serving plates.

Presentation:

Pour 2 tbsp of tomato butter sauce on the top periphery of the plate and arrange 3 kofta halves over it. Place crisp spinach leaves on one side of the plate and arrange 4 carrot buds around it. Place a mould of chick pea biryani on the opposite side. Pour 2 tbsp creamy dal and 2 tbsp saffron sauce around the dal.

Tasty Treat

Yield: 4 portions

Cottage cheese coins in spinach gravy. Stir-fried vegetable sticks with black pepper. Green pea and mushrooms in a creamy tomato sauce. Tasty pulao with potato-stuffed fried green chillies served with methi poori *fried to perfection.*

Ingredients:

For the vegetables with peppercorns:

Carrots *(gajar)*, serrated (2¼"x½"x½"), cooked	12/2¾ oz/75 gm
Potatoes, serrated (2¼"x½"x½"), cooked	12/2¾ oz/75 gm
Ghee	1 tbsp
Turmeric *(haldi)* powder	a pinch
Red chilli powder	a pinch
Cumin *(jeera)* powder	a pinch
Salt to taste	
Cashew/*Shahi* sauce (see p.17)	8 tbsp
Black peppercorns *(sabut kali mirch)*, crushed	½ tsp
Fennel *(saunf)* powder	a pinch
Lemon *(nimbu)* juice	1 tsp

For the flaky shell:

Flour *(maida)*	2½ tbsp
Ghee	½ tsp
Carom seeds *(ajwain)*	a pinch
Salt to taste	
Groundnut oil for deep-frying	

For the mushroom filling:

Mushrooms, blanched, sliced	1 oz/28 gm
Green peas *(mutter)*, blanched	½ oz/14 gm
Ghee	1 tbsp
Onion, sliced	1 tbsp
Ginger-garlic *(adrak-lasan)* paste	½ tsp
Green chillies, chopped	a pinch
Red chilli powder	a pinch
Salt to taste	
Tomatoes, chopped	5 tsp
Tomato butter sauce (see p.16)	3 tbsp
Green coriander *(hara dhaniya)*, chopped	1 tsp
Fenugreek *(methi)* powder	a pinch

For the cottage cheese coins:

Cottage cheese *(paneer)*, 1¾" diameter x ¼" thick	8/4 oz/120 gm
Saffron sauce (see p.18)	4 tbsp
Cardamom *(elaichi)* powder	a pinch
Fennel powder	a pinch
Spinach sauce (see p.18)	16 tbsp

Pulao (see p.106)	11 oz/320 gm
Green peas, boiled, sautéed	1 oz/28 gm
Tomato butter sauce	4 tbsp
Stuffed green chillies (see p.55)	4

Procedure:

- **For the vegetables with peppercorns:** Heat the ghee in a pan; add the spices and stir. Add the vegetables, cashew sauce, and salt; simmer for 1-2 minutes. Sprinkle black pepper, fennel powder, and lemon juice; stir.
- **For the flaky shell:** Make a hard dough with flour, ghee, carom seeds, salt, and 2 tsp water; keep aside for 10 minutes. Divide the dough into 4 equal portions and roll each into a disc (3" diameter). Line the disc into a greased plain mould (2¼" diameter x ¾" deep); prick and deep-fry the shells along with the mould until golden brown. Remove the fried shell gently.
- **For the filling:** Heat the ghee in a pan; sauté the onion until golden brown. Add ginger-garlic paste, green chillies, and red chilli powder; stir. Add tomatoes and cook for 1-2 minutes. Add mushrooms and green peas; sauté for a minute. Add tomato butter sauce; stir. Add coriander and fenugreek powder and stir. Divide the mixture into 4 equal portions and fill in the flaky shells.
- **For the cottage cheese coins:** Heat the saffron sauce, add the cottage cheese coins and simmer for 1-2 minutes. Sprinkle cardamom and fennel powders; stir. Heat the spinach sauce. Adjust the sauce consistency.
- Mix pulao with green peas. Divide the pea pulao into 4 equal portions and fill in the moulds. Steam for a minute and demould each on serving plates.

Presentation:

Place a mould of pea pulao in the centre of the serving plate. Arrange 3 pairs of carrot and potatoes with crushed peppercorn on one side and pour 1 tbsp of tomato butter sauce on the other side. Place the flaky mushroom and pea stuffed flaky shell on the sauce. Place a stuffed green chilli on top of the plate. Pour 2 tbsp of spinach sauce on the bottom periphery and place 2 cottage cheese coins dipped in saffron sauce over the sauce.(See photograph on p.70)

High Interest

Yield: 4 portions

A tempting spread sure to whet your appetite! Lamb coins in rogni *sauce. Delicious chicken dumplings in saffron sauce and aubergine quenelles served with pine nut and spinach pulao, spicy mashed potatoes, dal and* roomali roti.

Ingredients:

For lamb coins in *rogni* sauce:

Lamb leg, boneless cut into 2 thin escalopes	10½ oz/300 gm
Ginger-garlic *(adrak-lasan)* paste	2 tsp
Papaya paste (optional)	1 tbsp
Egg, beaten	¼
Cinnamon *(dalchini)* powder	½ tsp
Green coriander *(hara dhaniya)*, chopped	½ tbsp
Seasoning to taste	
Rogni sauce (see p. 17)	16 tbsp
Aromatic garam masala (see p.12)	a pinch

For the chicken dumplings in saffron sauce:

Chicken dumplings, cooked (see p.40)	12
Saffron sauce (see p.18)	16 tbsp
Fennel *(saunf)* powder	a pinch

For the aubergine quenelles:

Aubergines, diced into 1/3" pieces, deep-fried	4 oz/120 gm
Ghee	4 tsp
Garlic paste	1 tsp
Ginger, finely chopped	½ tsp
Green chillies, finely chopped	½ tsp
Onions, diced into 1/3" pieces	1 oz/28 gm
Tomatoes, diced into 1/3" pieces	3 oz/80 gm
Red chilli powder	a pinch
Cumin *(jeera)* powder	½ tsp
Green coriander, chopped	1 tsp
Salt to taste	

For the spicy potatoes:

Potatoes, boiled, mashed	1.1 lb/500 gm
Butter	2 tbsp
Cream	4 tbsp
Green chillies, finely chopped	1 tsp
Green coriander, chopped	1 tsp
Seasoning to taste	

For pine nut and spinach pulao:

Pulao (see p.106)	11 oz/320 gm
Pine nuts, fried	1 oz/28 gm
Crisp spinach (see p.13)	1 tbsp

Masala dal (see p.107)	6 tbsp
Tomato butter sauce (see p.16)	4 tbsp

Procedure:

- **For the lamb coins in *rogni* sauce:** Spread the escalopes on greased silver foils. Apply the ginger-garlic paste, papaya paste (optional) and egg on top. Sprinkle seasoning, cinnamon powder, and green coriander; keep aside for 30 minutes. Roll tightly with the foil. Tighten both the ends and make 2 8"-long rolls. Place the lamb rolls in a steamer and cook for 45 minutes or until cooked. Remove the foil, trim the sides and cut into 1" pieces. Heat the *rogni* sauce; add aromatic garam masala and the lamb coins. Simmer for 2-3 minutes. Adjust sauce consistency.
- **For the chicken dumplings in saffron sauce:** Bring the saffron sauce to the boil; add fennel powder and the chicken dumplings. Simmer for 2-3 minutes. Adjust the sauce consistency.
- **For the aubergine quenelles:** Heat the ghee in a pan; add garlic paste and sauté. Add ginger and green chillies, stir. Add onions and sauté over low heat until light brown. Add tomatoes, fried aubergines, red chilli powder, and cumin powder; stir. Add salt and cook for 1-2 minutes. Add green coriander and stir. Remove, divide into 4 portions and make quenelles with the help of 2 tbsp dipped in water.
- **For the spicy potatoes:** Mix the mashed potatoes with the remaining ingredients and make a smooth creamy mixture. (Yield: 1.1 lb/500 gm)
- **For pine nut and spinach pulao:** Mix the pulao with pine nuts and crisp spinach. Divide into 4 portions and fill in the moulds. Steam for a minute and demould on the serving plates.

Presentation:

Pipe two fancy spicy potato lines ¾″ apart at an angle on the serving plate. Fill the space in between with masala dal and pour ½ tbsp tomato butter sauce on both the ends of the masala dal. Arrange 3 pieces of lamb coins on one side and pour the sauce over them. Similarly, arrange 3 chicken dumplings on the top of the plate and cover with saffron sauce. Place an aubergine quenelle on one side of the piped potatoes and the pine nut and spinach rice mould on the other side with the lamb coins.

Double Feast

Yield: 4 portions

Chicken simmered in saffron sauce. Lamb and vegetables in rogni *sauce served with crisp spinach and tomato concasse.*

Ingredients:

For the chicken in saffron sauce:

Chicken, cut into ¼" cubes, steamed	5½ oz/160 gm
Saffron sauce (see p.18)	16 tbsp
Fennel *(saunf)* powder	½ tsp
White pepper *(safed mirch)*	a pinch
Aubergines *(baingan)*, medium-sized, halved, scooped, deep-fried	2/10 oz/280 gm

For the lamb and vegetables:

Rogni sauce (see p.17)	16 tbsp
Lamb, cut into ¼" cubes, steamed	4 oz/120 gm
Vegetables, cut into ¼" cubes, boiled	2¼ oz/60 gm
Cinnamon *(dalchini)* powder	a pinch
Cardamom *(elaichi)* powder	a pinch
Aubergines, medium-sized, halved, scooped, deep-fried	2/10 oz/280 gm

For the spinach moulds:

Spinach *(palak)*, blanched	3 oz/80 gm
Aubergine mixture (see p.85)	5½ oz/160 gm
Carrot flowers, blanched (see p.123)	4

Pulao (see p.106)	11 oz/320 gm
Tomato concasse	3 tbsp
Creamy dal (see p.107)	8 tbsp

Procedure:

- **For the chicken in saffron sauce:** Bring the saffron sauce to the boil; add chicken cubes and simmer for 2-3 minutes. Sprinkle fennel powder and white pepper; stir. Adjust the sauce consistency. Divide into 4 equal portions and fill in the fried aubergine cups.
- **For the lamb and vegetables:** Bring the *rogni* sauce to the boil; add lamb and vegetable cubes and simmer for 3-4 minutes. Add cinnamon and cardamom powders; stir. Adjust the sauce consistency. Divide into 4 equal portions and fill in the fried aubergine cups.
- **For the spinach moulds:** Line the moulds (2" diameter and 1" height) with spinach leaves and fill in 3 tbsp of the aubergine mixture; steam and demould. Arrange a carrot flower on top.
- **For the tomato pulao:** Mix the pulao with the tomato concasse. Divide into 4 equal portions and fill in the moulds. Steam for a minute and demould on the serving plate.

Presentation:

Arrange the chicken-filled aubergine cup and the lamb and vegetable-filled aubergine cup on the top of the serving plate. Place a tomato rice mould on the bottom of the plate and arrange the spinach mould and 2 tbsp of creamy dal on either side of the rice mould.

Triple Sensation

Yield: 4 portions

Chicken cutlet with tangy tomato sauce. Lamb cooked with dal. Mushroom filled spinach mould served with brown rice. Potato flower in a sour yoghurt sauce and missi roti.

Ingredients:

For the chicken cutlets:

Chicken mince	3 oz/80 gm
Ghee	2 tsp
Onion, chopped	1 tbsp
Green chillies, chopped	½ tsp
Turmeric *(haldi)* powder	a pinch
Cumin *(jeera)* powder	a pinch
Green coriander *(hara dhaniya)*, chopped	½ tbsp
Salt to taste	
Cornflour to dust	
Fresh breadcrumbs for coating	
Egg, beaten	½
Butter for shallow frying	
Tomato butter sauce (see p.16)	16 tbsp
Tomato chilli sauce	1 tbsp
Tomato ketchup	1 tbsp

For the lamb with dal:

Lamb coins (see p.85)	12
Masala dal, purée, (see p.107)	16 tbsp
Ghee	1 tsp
Aromatic garam masala (see p.12)	½ tsp
Lemon *(nimbu)* juice	1 tsp

For the spinach moulds:

Spinach, blanched	3 oz/80 gm
Ghee	4 tsp
Onions, chopped	2 tbsp
Red chilli powder	a pinch
Spinach, blanched, chopped	7 oz/200 gm
Mushrooms, boiled, sliced	2 oz/56 gm
Cumin powder	a pinch
Dry fenugreek *(kasoori methi)* powder	a pinch
Mango powder *(amchur)*	a pinch
Salt to taste	

For the potato flowers:

Potato flowers,boiled (see p.123)	4 (1½ oz/40 gm each)
Sour yoghurt sauce (see p.16)	16 tbsp
Cardamom *(elaichi)* powder	a pinch
White pepper *(safed mirch)*	a pinch

Brown rice (see p.106)	11 oz/320 gm
Spicy potatoes (see p.85)	

Procedure:

- **For the chicken cutlets:** Heat the ghee; sauté onion and chillies over medium heat until transparent. Add spices, green coriander, and salt; mix well. Remove and cool; mix with chicken mince. Divide into 4 equal portions and make flat round cutlets. Chill, dust with cornflour, dip in egg and coat with breadcrumbs. Shallow fry the cutlets until cooked. Heat the tomato butter sauce; add remaining ingredients and stir. Simmer the cutlets in the sauce for 2-3 minutes. Adjust consistency.
- **For the lamb with dal:** Boil the dal purée with 4 tbsp water. Add lamb coins and simmer. Heat the ghee; add aromatic garam masala, dal mixture, and lemon juice, stir. Adjust the sauce consistency.
- **For the spinach moulds:** Line 4 greased moulds with spinach leaves. Heat the ghee in a pan; sauté the onions until golden brown. Add red chilli powder and stir. Add spinach and cook for 2-3 minutes. Add the remaining ingredients; stir for a minute. Divide the mixture into 4 equal portions. Put a portion in the lined mould, steam for a minute and demould.
- **For the potato flowers:** Heat the sauce; add the potato flowers and simmer for 1-2 minutes. Sprinkle cardamom powder and white pepper powder; stir gently. Adjust the sauce consistency.

Presentation:

Arrange steamed brown rice mould in the centre of the serving plate. Pipe potato masala mixture as shown. Arrange 3 pieces of lamb coins and pour the dal mixture over them. Arrange a chicken cutlet and a spinach mould on either side of rice mould. Place a potato flower soaked with saffron sauce at the bottom of the plate.

Culinary Treat

Yield: 4 portions

Chicken rolls in a buttery tomato sauce and cubed lamb on spinach leaves served with masala dal, potato coins and moulds of trio pulao accompanied with cheese kulcha.

Ingredients:

For chicken in tomato butter sauce:

Chicken, 4 legs boneless, 2 legs placed together, flattened thin	1 lb/450 gm
Ginger-garlic *(adrak-lasan)* paste	1 tsp
Egg, beaten	½
Nutmeg *(jaiphal)* powder	½ tsp
Mango powder *(amchur)*	½ tsp
Seasoning to taste	
Green coriander *(hara dhaniya)*, chopped	½ tbsp
Tomato butter sauce (see p.16)	16 tbsp

For the lamb masala:

Ghee	4 tsp
Lamb, cut into ½″ cubes, boiled or steamed	3½ oz/100 gm
Onions, sliced	2 oz/56 gm
Ginger-garlic paste	1 tsp
Coriander powder	½ tsp
Red chilli powder	a pinch
Ginger, finely chopped	½ tsp
Green chillies, finely chopped	½ tsp
Tomato purée, fresh	½ cup
Green coriander, chopped	1 tsp
Cardamom *(elaichi)* powder	a pinch
Cinnamon *(dalchini)* powder	a pinch
Salt to taste	
Spinach, blanched	2 oz/56 gm
Butter	2 tsp

For potato coins in pepper sauce:

Potatoes, cut into cylinders (1½″ diameter, ½″ thick), steamed	7 oz/200 gm
Cashew/*Shahi* sauce (see p.17)	16 tbsp
Black peppercorns *(sabut kali mirch)*, crushed	½ tsp
Masala dal (see p.107)	8 tbsp

For the trio pulao:

Tomato pulao (see p.87)	4 oz/120 gm
Pea pulao (see p.82)	4 oz/120 gm
Saffron pulao (see p.79)	4 oz/120 gm

Procedure:

- **For the chicken in tomato butter sauce:** Spread chicken on a greased silver foil and apply ginger-garlic paste and egg. Sprinkle nutmeg and ginger powders, seasoning, and green coriander. Roll the chicken with the foil and tighten both the ends to make 2 8″-long cylinders. Cook the rolls in a steamer for 30 minutes or until cooked. Remove the foil and trim the sides. Cut the rolls into 1½″ pieces.
- Heat the tomato butter sauce and simmer the chicken rolls for 1-2 minutes in the sauce. Adjust the sauce consistency.
- **For the lamb masala:** Heat the ghee in a pan; sauté onions over medium heat until golden brown. Add ginger-garlic paste, coriander and red chilli powders; stir. Add ginger, green chillies, and tomato purée; bring to the boil and cook for 2-3 minutes. Add lamb cubes and 8 tbsp vegetable stock. Add green coriander, cardamom and cinnamon powders, and salt; stir.
- Melt the butter in a pan; add spinach and seasoning; stir for 30 seconds.
- **For the potato coins:** Heat the cashew sauce; add potato coins and simmer for a minute. Sprinkle pepper and stir. Adjust consistency.
- **For the trio pulao:** Divide each pulao into 4 portions and fill in the small moulds. Steam for half a minute and demould.

Presentation:

Arrange the spinach leaves in a circle in the middle of the serving plate. Put the lamb masala in the centre of the spinach circle. Arrange 3 pulaos on the periphery of the plate at equal distance. Between the pulao moulds arrange chicken in tomato butter sauce, potato coins in peppercorn sauce, and masala dal separately.

Festive Fare

Yield: 4 portions

A unique composition. Lamb biryani with potato-stuffed green chillies. Chicken coins in a spicy herbed tomato sauce and stir-fried crisp okra with a wholesome dal goes well with mutter kulcha.

Ingredients:

For the chicken coins:

Chicken breasts	2
Ginger-garlic *(adrak-lasan)* paste	1 tsp
Turmeric *(haldi)* powder	a pinch
Salt to taste	
Chicken mince (see p.58)	7 oz/200 gm
Tomato butter sauce (see p.16)	16 tbsp
Crisp spinach (see p.13)	½ oz/14 gm
Cardamom *(elaichi)* powder	a pinch
Mace *(javitri)* powder	a pinch

For crisp okra:
(Yield: 5½ oz/160 gm)

Okra, julienned	9 oz/250 gm
Lemon *(nimbu)* juice	1 tsp
Aromatic tangy masala (see p.12)	1 tbsp
Cornflour	1 tbsp
Flour *(maida)*	1 tsp
Groundnut oil for deep-frying	

Lamb biryani (see p.104)	12 oz/350 gm
Masala dal (see p.107)	8 tbsp

For the fried chillies:

Stuffed green chillies (see p.55)	4

Procedure:

- **For the chicken coins:** Flatten the chicken breasts thin. Rub ginger-garlic paste, turmeric powder, and salt; keep aside for 30 minutes. Divide the chicken mince into 2 portions and place a portion in the centre of the breast. Place the breasts on a silver foil, roll, and tighten from the two ends to make a 5″-long cylinder. Steam the rolls for 30 minutes. Unwrap and cut each roll into ¾″ coins.
- Heat the sauce in a pan; add the chicken coins and simmer for 2-3 minutes. Add the crisp spinach, cardamom powder, and mace powder; stir. Adjust the sauce consistency.
- **For crisp okra:** Mix the okra with the remaining ingredients and deep-fry in hot oil twice, until golden brown and crisp. Remove and drain on paper towels.
- Divide the lamb biryani into 4 equal portions and fill in the moulds. Steam for a minute and demould on the serving plate.

Presentation:

Demould a portion of lamb biryani on the top periphery of the serving plate. Place a stuffed fried chilli near the biryani. Arrange 3 chicken coins on the bottom periphery and pour the sauce on top. On both sides of the biryani, put crisp okra and masala dal.

Gourmet Experience

Yield: 4 portions

Chicken drumsticks in pickle spices; lamb in a thick coconut gravy; potato flowers in red gravy with carrot ribbon masala served with pea pulao and methi poori.

Ingredients:

For spiced chicken drumsticks:

Chicken drumsticks, boneless, marinated	4 (10½ oz/300 gm)
Ginger-garlic paste	2 tsp
Chicken mince (see p.58)	4 oz/120 gm
Ghee	1 tbsp
Fennel *(saunf)* seeds	a pinch
Fenugreek seeds *(methi dana)*	a pinch
Cumin *(jeera)* seeds	a pinch
Onion seeds *(kalonji)*	a pinch
Mustard seeds *(rai)*	
Vinegar *(sirka)*	2 tsp
Cashew/*Shahi* sauce (see p.17)	20 tbsp
Green chillies, julienned	½ tsp
Salt and black pepper to taste	

For the lamb in coconut sauce:

Lamb coins (see p.85)	12
Groundnut oil	2 tsp
Curry leaves *(kadhi patta)*	8
Coconut *(nariyal)*, grated	½ oz/14 gm
Tomatoes, chopped	3 tbsp
Rogni sauce (see p.17)	16 tbsp
Fennel powder	a pinch

For the carrot ribbon masala:

Carrot ribbons, blanched, 5″ long, 1″ wide, 3 mm thick (see p.122)	24/7 oz/200 gm
Groundnut oil	2 tsp
Turmeric *(haldi)* powder	a pinch
Red chilli powder	a pinch
Cumin powder	a pinch
Saffron sauce (see p.18)	10 tbsp
Lemon *(nimbu)* juice	1 tsp
Salt to taste	

For the potato flowers :

Potato flowers, boiled (see p.123)	4 (1½ oz/40 gm each)
Rogni sauce	14 tbsp
Cardamom *(elaichi)* powder	a pinch

Pea pulao (see p.82)	11 oz/320 gm
Stuffed green chillies, fried (see p.55)	4

Procedure:

- **For spiced chicken drumsticks:** Marinate chicken with lemon juice, 2 tsp ginger-garlic paste, and salt for 1 hour. Fill the marinated chicken with chicken mince and roast in a moderately hot tandoor until cooked. Heat the ghee; add all the seeds and stir until they start crackling. Add vinegar and cashew sauce; bring to the boil. Strain, add green chillies and seasoning; stir. Add chicken drumsticks and simmer for 3-4 minutes.
- **For the lamb in coconut sauce:** Heat the oil; add curry leaves and coconut; stir for 2 minutes. Add tomatoes and cook for 1-2 minutes. Add *rogni* sauce and bring to the boil. Add lamb coins and simmer for a minute. Stir in fennel powder and adjust the sauce consistency.
- **For the carrot ribbons masala:** Heat the oil; add spices and stir. Add saffron sauce and carrot ribbons; cook for a minute on low heat. Sprinkle lemon juice and salt; mix.
- **For the potato flowers:** Heat the *rogni* sauce; add potato flowers and simmer for 2-3 minutes. Stir in cardamom powder.
- Fill the pea pulao into 4 moulds. Steam for a minute and demould on the serving plate.

Presentation:

Arrange a pea pulao mould in the centre of the plate. Place a potato flower with *rogni* sauce on top and arrange 6 carrot ribbons folded and overlapping on both sides of the potato flower. Arrange chicken drumsticks and lamb in coconut sauce at the bottom of the plate with a fried chilli in between.

accompaniments

Piaz Kali Mirch Roti

Yield: 4

Unleavened bread topped with onion and black pepper mixture.

Ingredients:

Wholewheat flour *(atta)*	3½ oz/100 gm
Salt to taste	
For the topping:	
Ghee	1 tbsp
Ginger *(adrak)*, finely chopped	1 tsp
Green chillies, finely chopped	1 tsp
Onions, grated, squeezed	6 tbsp
Black peppercorns *(sabut kali mirch)*, pounded	½ tsp
Green coriander *(hara dhaniya)*, chopped	2 tbsp
Salt to taste	

Procedure:

- Mix wholewheat flour with salt and about 4 tbsp water; knead to make a semi-hard dough. Divide the dough into 4 equal portions and roll each out into a 4½″ disc on a lightly floured surface.
- **For the topping:** Heat the ghee in a pan; add ginger and green chillies, sauté for 30 seconds over medium heat. Add onions and sauté for a minute. Remove, add black pepper, green coriander, and salt; mix well. Divide into 4 equal portions. Spread a portion over each disc. Press gently. Place the bread on a dry *gaddi* (padded cushion) with the topping side down and stick the bread on the periphery of a moderately hot tandoor. Cook till baked. Serve warm.

Pudina Mutter Roti

Yield: 4

Unleavened bread topped with green pea and mint mixture.

Ingredients:

Wholewheat flour	3½ oz/100 gm
Salt to taste	
For the topping:	
Ghee	1 tbsp
Ginger *(adrak)*, finely chopped	1 tsp
Green chillies, finely chopped	1 tsp
Green peas *(mutter)*, boiled, crushed	3¼ oz/90 gm
Mint *(pudina)*, chopped	2 tbsp
Cumin *(jeera)* powder	a pinch
Salt to taste	

Procedure:

- Mix wholewheat flour with salt and about 4 tbsp water; knead to make a semi-hard dough. Divide the dough into 4 equal portions and roll each out into a 4½″ disc on a lightly floured surface.
- **For the topping:** Heat the ghee in a pan; add ginger and green chillies; sauté for 30 seconds over medium heat. Add green peas and sauté for a minute. Remove, add mint, cumin powder, and salt; stir. Divide into 4 equal portions. Spread a portion over each disc. Press gently. Place the bread on a dry *gaddi* (padded cushion) with the topping side down and stick the bread on the periphery of a moderately hot tandoor. Cook till baked. Serve warm.

Urad Dal Roti

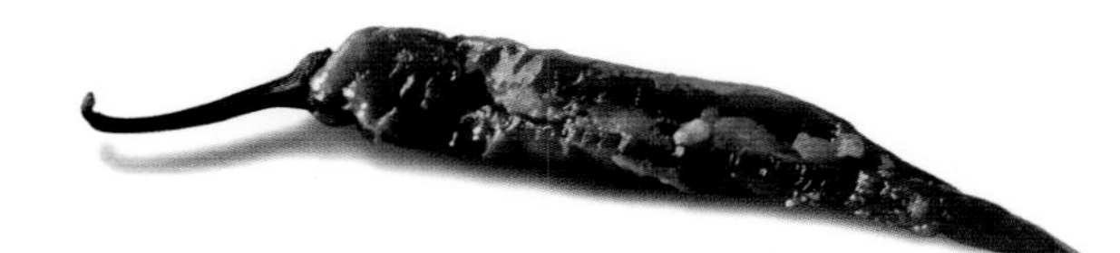

Yield: 4

Unleavened bread topped with black gram mixture.

Ingredients:

Wholewheat flour	3½ oz/100 gm
Salt to taste	
For the topping:	
Ghee	1 tbsp
Ginger *(adrak)*, finely chopped	1 tsp
Green chillies, finely chopped	1 tsp
Black gram *(dhuli urad dal)*, boiled with turmeric powder and salt, drained	2 oz/56 gm
Green coriander *(hara dhaniya)*, chopped	1 tbsp
Lemon *(nimbu)* juice	a few drops

Procedure:

- Mix wholewheat flour with salt and about 4 tbsp water; knead to make a semi-hard dough. Divide the dough into 4 equal portions and roll each out into a 4½″ disc on a lightly floured surface.
- **For the topping:** Heat the ghee in a pan; add ginger and sauté for 30 seconds over medium heat. Add green chillies and black gram; stir. Remove, add green coriander and lemon juice; mix well. Divide into 4 equal portions. Spread a portion over the disc. Press gently. Place the bread on a dry *gaddi* (padded cushion) with the topping side down and stick the bread on the periphery of a moderately hot tandoor. Cook till baked.
- Serve warm.

Kali Mirch Gajar Roti

Yield: 4

Unleavened bread topped with carrot and black pepper mixture.

Ingredients:

Wholewheat flour *(atta)*	3½ oz/100 gm
Salt to taste	
For the topping:	
Ghee	1 tbsp
Carrots *(gajar)*, grated	3¼ oz/90 gm
Black peppercorns *(sabut kali mirch)*, pounded	1 tsp
Lemon *(nimbu)* juice	a few drops

Procedure:

- Mix wholewheat flour with salt and about 4 tbsp water; knead to make a semi-hard dough. Divide the dough into 4 equal portions and roll each out into a 4½″ disc on a lightly floured surface.
- **For the topping:** Heat the ghee in a pan; add carrots and sauté for a minute over medium heat. Remove, add salt, black pepper, and lemon juice; sauté. Divide into 4 equal portions. Spread a portion over the disc. Press gently. Place the bread on a dry *gaddi* (padded cushion) with topping side down and stick the bread on the periphery of a moderately hot tandoor. Cook till baked.

Moong Dal Roti

Yield: 4

Unleavened bread topped with green gram and coriander mixture.

Ingredients:

Wholewheat flour *(atta)*	3½ oz/100 gm	Ginger *(adrak)*, finely chopped	1 tsp	Green coriander *(hara dhaniya)*, chopped	2 tbsp
Salt to taste		Green chillies, finely chopped	1 tsp	Cumin *(jeera)* powder	a pinch
For the topping:		Green gram *(moong dal)*, boiled, drained	3¼ oz/90 gm		
Ghee	1 tbsp				

Procedure:

- Mix wholewheat flour with salt and about 4 tbsp water; knead to make a semi-hard dough. Divide the dough into 4 equal portions and roll each out into a 4½″ disc on a lightly floured surface.
- **For the topping:** Heat the ghee in a pan; add ginger and green chillies; sauté for 30 seconds over medium heat. Add green gram and sauté for a minute. Remove, add green coriander, cumin powder, and salt; sauté. Divide into 4 equal portions. Spread a portion over the disc. Press gently. Place the bread on a dry *gaddi* (padded cushion) with the topping side down and stick the bread on the periphery of a moderately hot tandoor. Cook till baked. Serve warm.

Missi Roti

Yield: 4

Spicy unleavened gram flour bread.

Ingredients:

Gram flour *(besan)*	1 oz/28 gm	Salt to taste		Green chillies, finely chopped	1 tsp
Wholewheat flour *(atta)*	3¼ oz/90 gm	Ginger *(adrak)*, finely chopped	1 tsp	Onions, grated, squeezed	4 tsp
				Ghee	2 tsp

Procedure:

- Mix gram flour and flour with salt and the remaining ingredients. Pour melted ghee. Mix gradually and then add about ¼ cup water and knead to make a hard dough. Cover and keep aside for 30 minutes.
- Divide into 4 equal portions and roll each out into a 4½″ disc on a lightly floured surface. Spread a portion over the disc dusting with flour. Place the bread on a dry *gaddi* (padded cushion) and stick the bread on the periphery of a moderately hot tandoor. Cook till baked.
- Serve warm.

Roomali Roti

Yield: 4

Unleavened bread

Ingredients:

Wholewheat flour	2½ oz/70 gm	Flour *(maida)*	1 oz/28 gm	Salt to taste

Procedure:

- Mix wholewheat flour, flour, salt and about 4 tbsp water; knead to make a soft dough. Keep the dough aside for 10-15 minutes. Divide into 4 equal portions; shape into balls, and roll each out on a lightly floured surface into a round disc (approximately 9″). Place the disc on a convex griddle *(tawa)* and bake both sides.
- Serve warm.

Badami Naan

Yield: 4

Leavened bread flavoured with almonds.

Ingredients:

Flour *(maida)*	4¼ oz/125 gm	Egg, beaten	1/5	Groundnut oil	1 tsp
Salt to taste		Sugar	½ tsp	**For the topping:**	
Soda bicarbonate	a pinch	Yoghurt *(dahi)*, beaten	1 tsp	Almonds *(badam)*,	
Baking powder	a pinch	Milk	2 tsp	blanched, peeled, sliced	3 tbsp

Procedure:

- Mix flour, salt, soda bicarbonate, and baking powder together. Make a mixture with egg, sugar, yoghurt, and milk. Mix the flour with the egg mixture and knead to make a soft but smooth dough. Cover with a moist cloth and keep aside for 10 minutes. Add oil and punch the dough. Cover and keep aside for 1 hour to allow the dough to rise. Divide into 4 equal portions, make balls and roll each ball lightly into a 4½″ disc on a lightly floured surface. Apply little water on the surface.
- Divide the topping into 4 equal portions. Spread a portion on each disc. Press gently. Place the bread on a dry *gaddi* (padded cushion) with the topping side down and stick the bread on the periphery of a moderately hot tandoor. Cook till baked.
- Serve warm.

Dakkai Naan/Besani Laccha Naan

Yield: 4

A multi-layered leavened bread.

Ingredients:

Flour *(maida)*	3¼ oz/90 gm	Salt to taste		Milk	4 tsp
Gram flour *(besan)*	1 oz/28 gm	Fennel *(saunf)* powder	½ tsp	Yoghurt *(dahi)*, beaten	1 tsp
Baking powder	a pinch	Egg, beaten	1/5	Groundnut oil	1 tbsp
Soda bicarbonate	a pinch	Sugar	½ tsp	Butter, melted	2 tsp

Procedure:

- Mix flour, gram flour, baking powder, soda bicarbonate, salt, and fennel powder together. Make a mixture of egg, sugar, milk, and yoghurt. Mix the flour with the egg mixture together and knead to make a semi-hard dough. Cover with a moist cloth and keep aside for 10 minutes. Add oil and punch the dough. Cover and keep aside for 1 hour to allow the dough to rise. Divide into 4 equal portions. Flatten each into a 9″ round disc. Grease the surface with melted butter, dust with flour, hold from two ends and gather ensuring there are many folds. Roll it to make a ball *(pedah)* and then flatten into a 4½″ disc on a lightly floured surface. Place on a *gaddi* and stick the bread on the periphery of a moderately hot tandoor. Cook till baked. Serve warm.

Cheese Kulcha

Yield: 4

Leavened bread with vegetable topping.

Ingredients:

Flour *(maida)*	4 oz/120 gm	Yoghurt *(dahi)*, beaten	1 tsp	Tomatoes, brunoise	2 oz/56 gm
Salt and Soda bicarbonate	a pinch	Milk	2 tsp	Capsicum, brunoise	1½ oz/40 gm
Baking powder	a pinch	Groundnut oil	1 tsp	Green coriander *(hara dhaniya)*, chopped	2 tbsp
Egg, beaten	1/5	**For the topping:**		Salt to taste	
Sugar	½ tsp	Processed cheese, grated	5½ tbsp		

Procedure:

- Mix flour, salt, soda bicarbonate, and baking powder. Make a mixture with egg, sugar, yoghurt, and milk together. Mix flour with egg mixture and knead to make a soft but smooth dough. Cover with a moist cloth and keep aside for 10 minutes. Add oil and punch the dough. Cover and keep aside for 1 hour to allow the dough to rise. Divide into 4 equal portions, make balls and roll each ball into a 4½″ disc on a lightly floured surface.
- **For the topping:** Mix all the ingredients together. Divide into 4 equal portions. Spread a portion on each disc. Press gently. Place the bread on a dry *gaddi* (padded cushion) with the topping side touching the *gaddi* and stick the bread on the periphery of a moderately hot tandoor. Cook till baked. Serve warm.

Mutter Kulcha

Yield: 4

Leavened bread with green pea topping.

Ingredients:

Flour *(maida)*	4 oz/120 gm	Milk	2 tsp	Green peas *(mutter)*, boiled, crushed	3½ oz/100 gm
Salt to taste		Groundnut oil	1 tsp	Green coriander *(hara dhaniya)*, chopped	½ tbsp
Soda bicarbonate	a pinch	**For the topping:**		Mint *(pudina)*, chopped	½ tbsp
Baking powder	a pinch	Ghee	1 tbsp	Salt to taste	
Egg, beaten	1/5	Green chillies	1 tsp		
Sugar	½ tsp	Cumin *(jeera)* powder	½ tsp		
Yoghurt *(dahi)*, beaten	1 tsp				

Procedure:

- Mix flour, salt, soda bicarbonate, and baking powder. Make a mixture with egg, sugar, yoghurt, and milk. Mix flour with the egg mixture and knead to make a soft but smooth dough. Cover with a moist cloth and keep aside for 10 minutes. Add oil and punch the dough. Cover and keep aside for 1 hour to allow the dough to rise. Divide into 4 equal portions, make balls and roll each ball into a 4½″ disc dusting with flour. Apply little water on the surface.
- **For the topping:** Heat the ghee in a pan; add green chillies and stir. Add cumin powder, stir and then add green peas; stir for a minute over medium heat. Remove, add green coriander, mint, and salt; stir. Divide into 4 equal portions. Spread a portion on each disc. Press gently. Place the bread on a dry *gaddi* (padded cushion) with the topping side touching the *gaddi* and stick the bread on the periphery of a moderately hot tandoor. Cook till baked. Serve warm.

Methi Poori

Yield: 4

Deep-fried puffed bread flavoured with fenugreek.

Ingredients:

Wholewheat flour *(atta)*	3½ oz/100 gm	Dry fenugreek *(methi)* powder	1 tsp	Salt to taste
				Ghee for frying

Procedure:

- Mix flour, fenugreek, salt, and approximately 4 tbsp water; knead to make a tight dough. Keep aside for 30 minutes. Divide into 4 equal portions, make balls, apply little melted ghee on both sides of the balls and flatten each into 4½″ diameter.
- Heat the ghee in a pan; deep-fry the *poori* until golden brown. Serve warm.

Lamb Biryani

Yield: 4 portions

Flavoured lamb rice.

Ingredients:

Lamb, boneless, from leg cut into ¾″ cubes	9 oz/250 gm
Ghee	3½ tbsp
Onions, sliced	5 tbsp
Ginger-garlic *(adrak-lasan)* paste	5 tsp
Coriander *(dhaniya)* powder	1 tsp
Red chilli powder	1 tsp
Ginger, julienned	1 tsp
Green chillies, julienned	1 tsp
Tomato purée, fresh	10 tbsp
Mace-cardamom *(javitri-elaichi)* powder	½ tsp
Onions, sliced, browned	2 tsp
Mint *(pudina)*, chopped	1 tbsp
Green coriander *(hara dhaniya)*, chopped	3 tbsp
Lemon *(nimbu)* juice	1 tsp
For the yoghurt mixture:	
Yoghurt *(dahi)*	1 oz/28 gm
Cream	5 tbsp
Sugar *(breakfast)*	a pinch
Butter	5 tsp
Saffron *(kesar)*, dissolved in 2 tbsp water	½ gm
Salt to taste	
For the rice:	
Basmati rice, soaked for 30 minutes	9 oz/250 gm

Procedure:

- Heat the ghee in a pan; add onions and sauté over medium heat until golden brown. Add ginger-garlic paste, coriander powder, and red chilli powder (all dissolved in 4 tbsp water); stir for 2-3 minutes. Add lamb and sauté for another 2-3 minutes. Add tomato purée and half of the ginger and green chilli juliennes. Add approximately 2 cups water and cook the lamb over low heat until tender. Add half of mace- cardamom powder, stir, sprinkle browned onion, mint, green coriander, lemon juice, and remaining ginger and green chilli juliennes.
- **For the yoghurt mixture:** Mix yoghurt with the remaining mace-cardamom powder and the remaining ingredients. Pour half of this mixture over the lamb curry.
- **For the rice:** Boil approximately 3¾ cups water with salt. Add drained rice and boil over medium heat until ¾th cooked. Drain.
- **To assemble the biryani:** Spread the cooked rice over the prepared lamb curry and pour the remaining yoghurt mixture over the rice. Cover with butter paper and sprinkle some water over the butter paper. Seal the pan with silver foil and place in a moderately hot oven for 15 minutes. Remove.

Chick pea Biryani

Yield: 4 portions

Flavoured rice with chick peas.

Ingredients:

For the chick pea curry:

Chick peas *(kabuli chana)*	4¼ oz/125 gm
Soda bicarbonate	a pinch
Ghee	3½ tbsp
Onions, sliced	5 tbsp
Ginger-garlic *(adrak-lasan)* paste	5 tsp
Turmeric *(haldi)* powder	½ tsp
Red chilli powder	½ tsp
Coriander *(dhaniya)* powder	1 tbsp
Cumin *(jeera)* powder	½ tsp
Tomatoes, chopped	7 tbsp
Ginger, julienned	1 tsp
Green chilli, julienned	1 tsp
Yoghurt *(dahi)*	5 tbsp
Mace-cardamom *(javitri-elaichi)* powder	a pinch
Green coriander *(hara dhaniya)*, chopped	3 tbsp
Mint *(pudina)*, chopped	2 tsp
Saffron *(kesar)*, dissolved in 2 tbsp water	½ gm
Cream	½ cup
Butter	5 tsp
Salt to taste	

For the rice:

Basmati rice, soaked for 30 minutes	8 oz/225 gm
Salt to taste	

Procedure:

- **For the chick pea curry:** Soak chick peas for 2 hours. Drain. Put the chick peas in a pan, add water (approximately 4½ cups) and soda bicarbonate; cook until done. (Yield: 1 lb/450 gm along with the cooking liquid)
- Heat the ghee in a pan; add onions and sauté over medium heat until golden brown. Add ginger-garlic paste, turmeric powder, red chilli powder, coriander power, and cumin powder (all dissolved in 4 tbsp water) and stir for 2-3 minutes. Add tomatoes and cook until the clarified oil appears on the surface. Add half of the ginger and green chilli juliennes and yoghurt; stir. Now add boiled chick peas along with the liquid and cook for 2-3 minutes. Add half of the mace-cardamom powder. Sprinkle green coriander and mint, the remaining yoghurt and mace-cardamom powder, saffron, cream, and butter. Pour half of this mixture over the chick pea curry.
- **For the rice:** Boil water (approximately 3¾ cups), with salt and add the drained rice and boil over medium heat until ¾th cooked. Drain.
- **To assemble the biryani**: Spread the cooked rice over the prepared chick peas curry and pour the remaining yoghurt mixture over the rice. Cover the rice with butter paper and sprinkle some water over the butter paper. Seal the pan with silver foil and place the pan in a moderately hot oven for 15 minutes. Remove.

Brown Rice

Yield: 4 portions

Brown rice flavoured with ghee and onion.

Ingredients:

Basmati rice	14 oz/400 gm	Ghee	3½ tbsp	Onions, sliced, browned	7 tsp
Sugar	4 tsp	Salt to taste			

Procedure:

- Heat the sugar in a pan until it starts caramelizing. Add approximately 4¼ cups water and bring to the boil. Add ghee, stir, add the drained rice, salt, and browned onions; boil for 2 minutes. Reduce the heat and cook for another 2-3 minutes or until the water is absorbed by the rice. Cover the rice with butter paper and sprinkle some water over the butter paper. Seal the pan with a silver foil and place the pan in a moderately hot oven for 15 minutes. Remove.

Pulao

Yield: 4 portions

Rice cooked in vegetable stock.

Ingredients:

Basmati rice, soaked for 30 minutes	14 oz/400 gm	Carrots *(gajar)*, chopped	4¼ oz/125 gm	Onions, roughly chopped	2¼ oz/60 gm
Vegetable stock	4 cups	Celery, roughly chopped	3½ oz/100 gm	Green cardamoms *(choti elaichi)*	5
Ghee	3½ tbsp	Leeks, roughly chopped	2¼ oz/60 gm	Cloves *(laung)*	2
For the vegetable stock:				Cinnamon *(dalchini)* stick	1
Cauliflower	2¾ oz/75 gm			Cumin *(jeera)* seeds	½ tsp

Procedure:

- Boil the vegetable stock; add ghee, salt, and drained rice and boil for 2 minutes; reduce to medium heat and cook for another 2-3 minutes or until the stock is absorbed by the rice. Cover the rice with butter paper and sprinkle some water over the butter paper. Seal the pan with a silver foil and place the pan in a moderately hot oven for 15 minutes. Remove.
- **For the vegetable stock:** Add all the ingredients in a pan and approximately 16 cups water; bring to the boil and simmer for 1 hour. Remove and strain gently. (Yield: 4 cups)

Masala Dal

Yield: 4 portions

Spicy red gram dal

Ingredients:

Split red gram *(arhar dal)*	8 oz/225 gm
Turmeric *(haldi)* powder	½ tsp
Tomato purée	10 tbsp
Green chillies, chopped	1 tsp
Salt to taste	
For the tempering:	
Butter	3 tbsp
Onions, chopped	2 tbsp
Ginger-garlic *(adrak-lasan)* paste	2 tsp
Cumin *(jeera)* powder	1½ tsp
Red chilli powder	½ tsp
Tomatoes, chopped	7 tbsp
Green chillies, chopped	1 tsp
Green coriander *(hara dhaniya)*, chopped	1 tbsp
Lemon *(nimbu)* juice	1 tsp

Procedure:

- Boil the dal with 10 cups water and the remaining ingredients. Cook until tender. Mash lightly.
- **For the tempering**: Heat the butter in a frying pan; add onions and sauté over medium heat until golden brown. Add ginger-garlic paste, cumin powder, and red chilli powder; stir for a minute. Add tomatoes and sauté for 2-3 minutes, add green chillies and stir. Pour the boiled dal over and bring to the boil. Sprinkle green coriander and lemon juice; stir well.

Creamy Dal

Yield: 4 portions

Black gram flavoured with tomatoes and laced with cream.

Ingredients:

Black gram *(urad dal)*	7 oz/200 gm
Tomato purée	7 oz/200 gm
For the tempering:	
Butter	6 tbsp
Ginger-garlic *(adrak-lasan)* paste	6 tsp
Red chilli powder	½ tsp
Asafoetida *(hing)*, dissolved in 2 tsp water	a pinch
Cream	6 tbsp
Salt to taste	

Procedure:

- Soak the dal for 2 hours. Drain. Boil dal with 10 cups water until cooked. Do not stir the dal in between. Remove, mash lightly. Add tomato purée and 2½ cups water and bring to the boil.
- **For the tempering:** Heat the butter in a pan, add ginger-garlic paste and stir for a minute. Add red chilli powder and asafoetida; stir. Add the dal along with water and bring to the boil until the water has almost evaporated. Add cream, salt and boil for 2-3 minutes.

desserts

Kaleidoscope

Yield: 4 portions

A trio of colourful Indian halwas— *red carrot, almond, and white pumpkin— centred with rose-flavoured concentrated milk.*

Ingredients:

For the carrot *halwa*:
(Yield: 5½ oz/160 gm)

Red carrots *(lal gajar)*, grated	6¼ oz/175 gm
Water	5 tbsp
Sugar	7 tsp
Ghee	4 tsp
Wholemilk fudge *(khoya)*, grated	1¾ oz/50 gm
Cardamom essence or Cardamom powder	1-2 drops a pinch
Orange red colour (optional)	a few drops

For the white pumpkin *halwa*: (Yield: 5 oz/140 gm)

Pumpkin *(petha)*, grated	7 oz/200 gm
Water	5 tbsp
Sugar	7 tsp
Ghee	4 tsp
Wholemilk fudge *(khoya)*, grated	2 oz/56 gm
Cardamom essence or Cardamom powder	1-2 drops a pinch
Vetivier *(kewra)* essence	1-2 drops
Green colour (optional)	a few drops

For the almond *halwa*:
(Yield: 7 oz/200 gm)

Almonds *(badam)*, blanched, peeled	2¾ oz/75 gm
Milk	8 tbsp
Sugar	5½ tbsp
Saffron *(kesar)*	a pinch
Ghee	3½ tbsp

For the garnishing:

Rabdi (see p.112)	4 tbsp
Rose syrup	a few drops
Assorted fruits scoops (balls)	12

Procedure:

- **For the carrot *halwa*:** Put the carrots in a pan; add approximately 5 tbsp water and cook over medium heat until the water has evaporated. Add sugar and stir continuously until dissolved. Add ghee and sauté for 2-3 minutes. Add wholemilk fudge and stir for 2-3 minutes. Add cardamom essence and orange red colour and stir. Divide the *halwa* into 4 equal portions and make quenelles with the help of 2 tbsp dipped in hot water.
- **For the white pumpkin *halwa*:** Put the pumpkin in a pan, add approximately 5 tbsp water and cook over medium heat until the water has evaporated. Add sugar and continue stirring until dissolved. Add ghee and fry for 2-3 minutes. Add wholemilk fudge and stir for 2-3 minutes. Add cardamom and vetivier essences and green colour; stir. Divide the *halwa* into 4 equal portions and make quenelles with the help of 2 tbsp dipped in hot water.
- **For the almond *halwa*:** Put the almonds in a blender, add milk and make a purée. Melt the sugar in a pan over medium heat, add approximately ½ cup water and make a syrup of two string consistency. Add saffron and stir. Add almond paste and cook over low heat for 20 minutes or until semi-dry. Incorporate melted ghee, little at a time, and continue stirring till it leaves the sides of the pan. Divide the *halwa* into 4 equal portions and make quenelles with the help of 2 tbsp dipped in hot water.

Presentation:

Pipe a thin whipped cream line as shown in the photograph. Place a scoop of fruit on each edge. Fill the centre space with the rose *rabdi*. Arrange the 3 varieties of *halwa* quenelles on three sides.

Classic Harmony

Yield: 4 portions

The traditional sweet bread shahi tukra *blends perfectly with rich chocolate sauce. Round, juicy, soft centred sweets set off the well-flavoured guava compote.*

Ingredients:

For the bread *tukra*:

Refrigerated bread, cut into 2½″ squares and 1″ height	4 (7 oz/200 gm)
Groundnut oil for frying	

For the syrup:

Sugar syrup	1½ cups
Cardamom *(elaichi)* powder	1 tsp

For the *rabdi* (thickened milk*)*:

Milk	5 cups
Cornflour	½ oz/14 gm
Gelatin	½ tbsp

For the guava compote:

Guavas, sliced with skin, remove seeds	7 oz/200 gm
Sugar	7 tbsp
Bay leaf *(tej patta)*	1
Cinnamon *(dalchini)* sticks	2
Cloves *(laung)*	5

For the garnishing:

Sugar (for sugar stencil)	5¼ oz/150 gm
Truffle sauce (see below)	7 tbsp
Pistachio *(pista)* slivers	1 tbsp
Assorted fruit scoops (balls)	12

Procedure:

- **For the bread *tukra*:** Make a 1″ diameter and 3 mm deep incision in the centre of the bread squares with the help of a cutter. Heat the oil and fry the bread squares until golden brown. Remove and drain.
- **For the syrup:** Add cardamom powder to the warm syrup; mix well. Soak the fried bread into the syrup for a minute. Remove, drain and cool.
- **For the *rabdi*:** Heat the milk in a pan over medium heat and cook till it is reduced to half. Remove. Add cornflour (dissolved in ¼ cup milk) and stir until warm. Add gelatin (dissolved in 2 tbsp water), stir. Keep the container in an ice bath, stir till coating consistency. Soak the bread squares in the *rabdi*, remove and keep them inverted on a cooling rack; refrigerate.
- **For the guava compote:** Caramelize 4 tsp sugar in a pan over medium heat. Add guavas and cook for a minute. Add bay leaf, cinnamon sticks, cloves, and enough water to cook the guavas. Add the remaining sugar. Stir continuously until it is of syrupy consistency. Remove and divide into 4 equal portions; discard the spices.
- **For the garnishing:** Caramelize the sugar and pour over a silver foil in a zig-zag pattern. Cool and remove the stencils gently.
- **For the truffle sauce:** Boil 3½ tbsp cream in a thick-bottomed pan. Add 7 tbsp chocolate, cut into bits gradually. Stir and bring to the boil again. Remove, strain, cool and use as required.

Presentation:

Place the *shahi tukra* in the centre of a serving plate. Arrange a cutter in the incision and pour a portion of the truffle sauce in the incision. Remove the cutter gently. Spread the guava compote and the flavoured syrup around the *shahi tukra*. Arrange three fruit scoops at the top and sprinkle pistachio all around. Insert the sugar stencil in the centre of the *shahi tukra*.

Golden Fleece

Yield: 4 portions

A fennel-flavoured sweet pancake soaked in a tangy orange sauce delicately encased in a caramel cage.

Ingredients:

For the pancakes:

Semolina *(suji)*	½ oz/14 gm
Flour *(maida)*	4 tbsp
Water	1 cup
Wholemilk fudge *(khoya)*, mashed	3½ oz/100 gm
Fennel *(saunf)* powder	a pinch
Ghee for frying	

For the orange sauce:
(Yield: 1 cup see p.120)

For the sweet roses:
(Yield: 20 roses)

Flour	1¾ cups
Butter	3½ tbsp
Breakfast sugar	3 tbsp
Egg	1
Ghee for frying	
Sugar syrup (1 string consistency)	1 cup

For the spun sugar:

Sugar	7 oz/200 gm

For the garnishing:

Rabdi (see p.112) without gelatine	2¼ oz/60 gm
Fresh fruits, cut into fans	8
Mint *(pudina)*	8 sprigs

Procedure:

- **For the pancakes:** Mix semolina, flour, and water together. Soak for 5 minutes. Add wholemilk fudge and fennel powder; mix well. Divide the mixture into 4 equal portions. Heat the ghee in a flat pan; drop a portion of the batter and fry the pancake on low heat until golden brown on both sides. Remove and soak in the orange sauce for 5 minutes. Remove.
- In order to get a neat shape pancake, place a ring (3″ diameter) in the pan and then pour the batter in the ring. Remove the ring once the pancake is half done.
- **For the sweet roses:** Mix flour, butter, sugar, and egg; knead to make a hard dough. Divide the dough into small balls. Make a small bud with the small ball. Flatten a small ball with fingers making it thinner at the top. Stick this petal to the bud. Repeat the process 4 times by sticking the petal and overlapping each other. Curve the top of the petals towards outer side to resemble a rose. Heat the ghee and deep-fry the roses over low heat until golden brown. Remove and dip in the warm sugar syrup for 5 minutes. Remove.
- **For the spun sugar:** Melt the sugar over low heat until light golden brown. Remove and cool until thick. Place 3 long handled wooden spoons/palette knives/iron rods on a table. Dip a fork in the caramel and wave over the wooden spoons, etc., to get the sugar strings. Lift the sugar strings gently with both hands and place over the sweet pancake.

Note: If the caramel sets, re-heat again.

Presentation:

Place a pancake at the bottom periphery of a serving plate along with some sauce and cover with the spun sugar. Pour a spoonful of *rabdi* on the top periphery and place a sweet rose on top. Arrange 2 fruit fans on the sides and 2 mint sprigs on either side of the rose. (See photograph on p.108)

Treasured Moments

Yield: 6 portions

The all-time favourite pistachio kulfi *surrounded by black grape coulis and sweet 'n' sour mango sauce sprinkled with saffron flakes.*

Ingredients:

For the pistachio *kulfi*:

Milk (full cream) — 10 cups
Sugar — 4¼ oz/125 gm
Pistachios *(pista)*, peeled, sliced — 3½ oz/100 gm
Cream — ½ cup
Pistachio powder — 3½ tbsp
Cardamom *(elaichi)* powder — a pinch
Black grape coulis (see p.120) — 10½ oz/300 gm

For the mango sauce:

Mango purée — 1 cup
Sugar — 3½ tbsp

For the garnishing:

Saffron *(kesar)* flakes — a pinch
Falooda (also available in the market) — 5½ tbsp

Procedure:

- **For the pistachio *kulfi*:** Boil the milk on medium heat and cook till reduced to coating consistency. Add sugar and stir until dissolved. Add the remaining ingredients and stir. Remove and cool. Divide into 6 equal portions and pour each into a brioche mould. Cover with silver foil and freeze.
- **For the mango sauce:** Heat the mango purée over low heat; add sugar and continue stirring until the sauce starts bubbling.
- **For the *falooda*:** Mix 7 oz/200 gm cornflour with about 5 cups water and boil over medium heat, stirring constantly, until reduced to a gelatinous consistency with a sheen on the surface. Force the cooked cornflour immediately through a noodle press, using the 1/16″ mesh over a container filled with chilled water.

Presentation:

Spread a portion of the *falooda* in the centre of a serving plate and place the *kulfi* on top. Pour the black grape coulis around the *kulfi* and then pour the mango sauce around the black grape coulis. Sprinkle saffron flakes over the mango sauce.

Royal Orchard

Yield: 4 portions

A tasty rabdi *dariole garnished with nuts served on a spicy pepper crust and decorated with black pebbles.*

Ingredients:

For the *rabdi* dariole:

Milk	10 cups
Sugar	5¼ oz/150 gm
Gelatin	½ tbsp
Rose syrup	4 tsp
Cream, whipped	5 tbsp
Almonds *(badam)*, blanched, de-skinned, sliced	¾ oz/20 gm
Pistachios *(pista)*, blanched, de-skinned	¾ oz/20 gm
Raisins *(kishmish)*	¾ oz/20 gm
Almond flakes	½ oz/14 gm
Pistachio slivers	½ oz/14 gm

For the black pebbles:

Chenna (curdled milk with whey removed)	1 oz/28 gm
Wholemilk fudge *(khoya)*	3½ oz/100 gm
Flour *(maida)*	2 tbsp
Water	1 tbsp
Sugar syrup	1 cup
Ghee for frying	

For the pepper crusts: (Yield: 10 no.)

Flour *(maida)*	3½ oz/100 gm
Black peppercorns *(sabut kali mirch)*, crushed	1 tsp
Salt to taste	
Ghee	4 tsp
Water	8 tsp
Groundnut oil for frying	

For the garnishing:

Mango sauce (see p.115)	12 tbsp
Black grape coulis (see p.120)	2 tbsp
Pistachio slivers	1 tbsp

Procedure:

- **For the *rabdi* dariole:** Boil the milk in a flat pan over medium heat. Add sugar and stir continuously until the milk is reduced to a coating consistency. Remove and cool. Soak gelatin in 2 tbsp water and melt over a double boiler. Add melted gelatin and mix well. Add rose syrup and cream; mix gently. Dry roast the almonds and pistachios; add to the *rabdi* mixture along with the raisins. Divide the mixture into 4 portions. Pour a portion of the mixture into a ring cutter (2″ diameter and 1½″ height) and close from one side with a silver foil. Refrigerate. Demould, insert almond flakes overlapping at the edge of each dariole. Sprinkle pistachio slivers on the dariole.
- **For the black pebbles:** Grate wholemilk fudge, add *chenna* and rub on a table until smooth. Add flour and water and knead gently to make a soft dough. Divide the mixture into 36 tiny portions and shape into pebbles. Heat the ghee on slow heat; add the pebbles and fry until black. Remove and transfer to warm syrup for 3-4 minutes. Remove and drain.
- **For the pepper crusts:** Mix the flour with pepper and salt; add melted ghee and rub in to make the mixture crumbly. Add water and knead to make a tight dough. Divide the dough into 10 portions, roll and shape each into a 2 mm thick disc. Cut with a cutter (3″ diameter). Prick and deep-fry in oil until golden brown and crisp.

Presentation:

Place the pepper crust disc in the centre of a serving plate. Arrange the *rabdi* dariole over it. Place a set of 3 pebbles in 3 corners of the plate at equal distance and arrange mint sprigs on each set of pebbles. Pour 3 tbsp mango coulis in between the pebble sets. Pour 1 tsp of black grape coulis over the mango coulis and run a fork on the coulis to make a design.

Paan Sorbet

Yield: 2.2 lb

The after meal digester, paan, *transformed into a delicious minty ice cream.*

Ingredients:

Water	5 cups	*Paan* liqueur	10 tbsp	Orange red colour	1 tsp
Sugar	6¼ oz/175 gm	Egg white	1	Mint *(pudina)*	4 sprigs

Procedure:

- Put water and sugar into a pan and bring to the boil over medium heat. Remove, cool and chill over ice bath. Add the *paan* liqueur, egg white, and orange red colour; mix well. Put the mixture in a sorbet-making machine and churn until fluffy. Remove and freeze.

Presentation:

Scoop out a portion, arrange in a serving glass cup and garnish with a mint sprig. Serve immediately.

Sweet Symphony

Yield: 4 portions

A daring experiment; crushed black peppercorns and cardamom ice cream. Crunchy fennel and pistachio sugar-crusted flour noodles enriched with black grape and orange sauce.

Ingredients:

For the noodles:

Flour *(maida)*	3½ oz/100 gm
Ghee	1 tbsp
Water	2 tbsp
Groundnut oil for frying	
Sugar syrup (single string consistency)	2½ cups
Fennel *(saunf)* powder	1 tbsp
Pistachios *(pista)*, blanched,de-skinned, chopped	1 tbsp

For black pepper ice cream:
(Yield: 2.2 lb/1 kg)

Black peppercorns *(sabut kali mirch)*, crushed	1½ tbsp
Egg yolks	10
Cream	4 cups
Sugar	7 oz/200 gm

For the cardamom ice cream:
(Yield: 2.2 lb/1 kg)

Green cardamom *(choti elaichi)* powder	1 tbsp
Egg yolks	10
Sugar	5¼ oz/150 gm
Cream	4 cups

For the black grape coulis:
(Yield: 10 oz/280 gm)

Black grapes, seedless	9 oz/250 gm
Sugar	3 tbsp
Lemon *(nimbu)* juice	a few drops
Water	3½ tbsp
Créme de casis	2 tbsp

For the orange sauce:
(Yield: 7 oz/200 gm)

Orange juice	2½ cups
Sugar	3½ tbsp
Cointreau	2 tbsp
Orange powder (dry orange skin, crushed into powder)	½ tsp

Procedure:

- **For the noodles:** Melt the ghee and rub into the flour. Add warm water and knead to make a hard dough. Roll into 1 mm thickness. Cut lengthwise into strips. Make a bunch of strips and place them in a wire mesh (strainer). Fry it along with the mesh till golden brown. Remove.
- Boil the sugar syrup; add fennel powder and stir. Dip the crispy strips in the sugar syrup, sprinkle chopped pistachio and keep aside.
- **For the black pepper ice cream:** Whip the yolks and sugar till fluffy, add cream. Cook in the double boiler till coating consistency; cool and churn in the ice cream machine along with peppercorns for 30 minutes. Remove and freeze.
- **For the cardamom ice cream:** Whip the yolks and sugar till fluffy, add cream. Cook in the double boiler till coating consistency; cool and churn in the ice cream machine with cardamom powder for 30 minutes. Remove and freeze.
- **For the black grape coulis:** Cook the grapes, water, sugar, and lemon juice pressing the grapes with a wooden spoon. Cook till coating consistency. Cool, add créme de casis and stir. Strain some coulis and reserve the sauce to be used during presentation.
- **For the orange sauce:** Boil the orange juice with sugar and cook over low heat until coating consistency. Cool, add Cointreau and orange powder; stir.

Presentation:

Spread the black grape coulis in the centre of the plate. Place the crispy bunch over the coulis. Arrange a scoop each of the black pepper ice cream and cardamom ice cream over it. Pick any spiral from the bunch and place it over the scoop. Pour orange sauce and black grape coulis in circles adjacent to each other. Run a fork between them. Serve chilled.

vegetable shapes

tomato & lemon rosettes

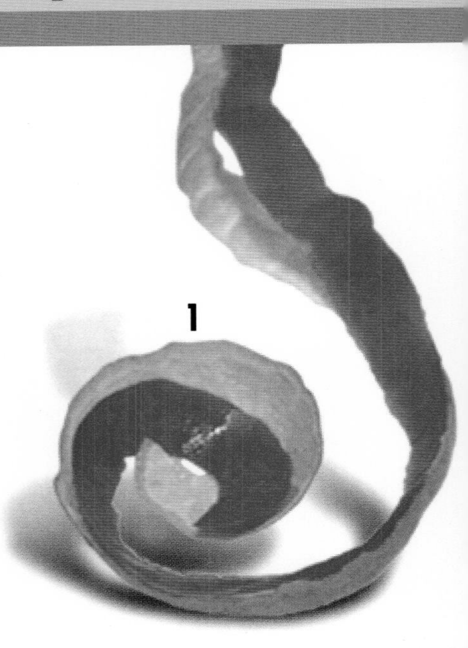

STEP 1
Take a firm red tomato and peel the skin with the help of a small, sharp knife in a circular fashion, taking off only the thick skin without breaking it at any point.

STEP 2
Fold the skin with flesh side inside in a spiral manner. Make sure that once folded the rosettes rests comfortably on the base or end of the peeled tomato.

Do the same for the Lemon Rosette.

STEP 1
To prepare lemon and tomato rosette, join two long peeled strips of tomato and lemon.

STEP 2
Fold in the same fashion as above forming a rosette.

2

carrot ribbons

STEP 1
Peel an even-sized broad red carrot and cut the eye part.

STEP 2
Slice the carrot lengthwise in a slicing machine (3 mm thick).

potato flower

2

STEP 1
Take a medium-sized potato, make a base by taking off a small slice at any end.

STEP 2
Shape the potato by peeling off the skin from the base end in a circular manner so as to form a stand that converges to the base.

3

STEP 3
With the tip of a small knife, make an incision of 1 cm deep in a circular manner. Repeat along the same incision of 3 mm thickness to make a petal.

4

STEP 4
In the same manner, make 3 more petals at the base end of the potato.

STEP 5
Now carve more petals keeping in mind that each petal must be carved between two petals.

5

carrot flowers

STEP 1
Peel a medium-sized red carrot. Make deep groves vertically.

1

STEP 2
Cut into (3 mm thick) slices.

2

tomato/lemon wings

STEP 1
Take a firm red tomato and with the help of a sharp, small knife make a 45° incision of 3 mm depth from both sides to form a "V" shape in the centre. Remove the top part and keep aside.

STEP 2
Repeat the procedure 3 times, leaving 3 mm space on both the sides. Keep removing the wings.

STEP 3
Place wings one on top of the other starting with the largest to the smallest. Push each wing forward with 3 mm space.

Do the same for the lemon wings.

carrot buds

STEP 1
Peel an even medium-sized red carrot. Cut 4 vertical slants keeping the narrow end at the bottom; just like one sharpens a pencil.

STEP 2
Along the 4 vertical slants, cut the carrot thinly keeping the base joined. Keep in mind that all 4 cuts are joined together with the tip of the knife.

STEP 3
Push the bottom pointed end of the carrot so that the bud is released keeping all the 4 sides intact.

Continue the same procedure to make more carrot buds till you reach to the thicker part of the carrot.

easy menus

MENU 1

VEGETARIAN

STEAMED RICE CAKE (see p.25)

GRAM FLOUR PANCAKE WITH VEGETABLE KEBAB (see p.55)
ONION & PEPPER ROTI (see p.98)

SPICED COTTAGE CHEESE IN HERBED TOMATO SAUCE (see p.75)
PINE NUT PULAO (see p.73)
SPINACH MOULD WITH DAL (see p.75)
POTATO BALLS IN SAFFRON SAUCE (see p.75)

ROSE RABDI DARIOLE (see p.116)

MENU 2

VEGETARIAN

TOMATO SOUP WITH GREEN PEA TIMBALE (see p.23)

BENGAL GRAM CAKE WITH TOMATO CHUTNEY (see p.57)
CARROT & PEPPER ROTI (see p.99)

COTTAGE CHEESE & CARROT BALLS IN SAFFRON SAUCE (see p.77)
PEA PULAO (see p.82)
TOMATO CUP (see p.77)
VEGETABLE SPINACH MOULD (see p.77)

FENNEL AND ORANGE SWEET PANCAKE (see p.113)

MENU 3

NON-VEGETARIAN

CHICKEN DUMPLINGS (see p.40)

TURMERIC CHILLI POMFRET (see p.62)
MINT AND GREEN PEA ROTI (see p.98)

LAMB COINS IN ROGNI SAUCE (see p.85)
CRISP SPINACH PULAO (see p.73)
AUBERGINE QUENELLES (see p.85)
MASALA DAL (see p.107)

ALMOND QUENELLES (see p.110)

MENU 4

NON-VEGETARIAN

LAMB BROTH (see p.34)

SPIRAL FISH ROLL (see p.68)
MOONG DAI ROTI (see p.100)

CHICKEN CUTLET WITH TANGY TOMATO SAUCE
(see p.88)
BROWN RICE (see p.106)
MUSHROOM SPINACH MOULD (see p.88)
POTATO FLOWER (see p.88)
SOUR YOGHURT SAUCE (see p.16)

PISTACHIO KULFI WITH BLACK GRAPE COULIS
(see p.115)

index

Accompaniments

BREADS

BIRYANI AND RICE

DAL

Desserts